King's High School

PRIZE AWARD

Name ...... **Jared Fudge** ......

For ...... **Excellence in 2 subjects** ......

Principal ....

KHS

Call of the River

Viking

Published by the Penguin Group
Penguin Books Australia Ltd
250 Camberwell Road, Camberwell, Victoria 3214, Australia
Penguin Books Ltd
80 Strand, London WC2R 0RL, England
Penguin Putnam Inc.
375 Hudson Street, New York, New York 10014, USA
Penguin Books Canada Limited
10 Alcorn Avenue, Toronto, Ontario, Canada M4V 3B2
Penguin Books (N.Z.) Ltd
Cnr Rosedale and Airborne Roads, Albany, Auckland, New Zealand
Penguin Books (South Africa) (Pty) Ltd
24 Sturdee Avenue, Rosebank, Johannesburg 2196, South Africa
Penguin Books India (P) Ltd, 11, Community Centre, Panchsheel Park
New Delhi 110 017, India

First published by Penguin Books Australia, 2002

Copyright © Philip Weigall, 2002
Illustrations copyright © Trevor Hawkins, 2002

10 9 8 7 6 5 4 3 2

All rights reserved. Without limiting the rights under copyright reserved above, no part of this publication may be reproduced, stored in or introduced into a retrieval system, or transmitted in any form or by any means (electronic, mechanical, photocopying, recording or otherwise) without the prior written permission of both the copyright owner and the above publisher of this book.

Designed by Cathy Larsen, Penguin Design Studio
Illustrations by Trevor Hawkins
Typeset in 11.25/16 Sabon by Post Pre-press Group, Brisbane, Queensland
Scanning by Splitting Image P/L, Blackburn, Victoria
Printed and bound by McPherson's Printing Group, Maryborough, Victoria

National Library of Australia
Cataloguing-in-Publication data

Weigall, Philip.
Call of the river: Australian and New Zealand fly-fishing adventures.

ISBN 0 670 04065 7.

1. Fly fishing – New Zealand. 2. Fly fishing – Australia. 3. Australia – Description and travel.
4. New Zealand – Description and travel. I. Hawkins, Trevor. II. Title.

799.1240993

www.penguin.com.au

Call of the River

Philip Weigall

Illustrated by Trevor Hawkins

VIKING

Foreword

A WET SUMMER. Sheep are hidden beneath the swathes of green lucerne. Country back roads hum beneath a haze of insects. My friend Patrick Hughes and I drive through eucalypt forests and old goldmining towns, devouring home-made pasties and contemplating trout.

Philip Weigall's house squats neatly on a hill. Scattered inside the house are loose photographs of a lean man, in some alone, in some huddled with other men wearing checkered shirts and polaroid glasses, standing by watercourses, nestling fly-fishing rods. In each he cradles an outsized trout. Massive, arching brown trout. Four pounders. Eight pounders. Rainbow trout still glistening and hooked. Preposterous trout.

Look at the man holding the fish. See the impish enthusiasm and the stillness within him. See in the photographs his genuine delight yet lack of surprise. A man who knows with certainty he will catch vast trout but is gratified every time the inevitable confronts him and the fly is snatched and the reel whines.

I think to myself, Were these my fish, were I this man, these photographs would be cherished, enlarged beyond Brobdingnagian proportions, framed in mahogany and mounted over fireplaces, proclaiming my mastery over nature and fly lines. Instead, these snapshots adorn the back of a refrigerator, fastened by magnets, obscured by notices. There is humility to the man. These were yesterday's fish, and he itches for tomorrow's catch.

Patrick and I follow Philip to one of his favourite lakes, sunk deep in the chocolate soil near Ballarat. They're fussy he says. Big but fussy. To illustrate his point a massive trout leaps from the water, bangs and belly-flops like an FJ Holden dropped from a height, taunting us.

Philip gives us the low-down, shares his home-tied flies and, satisfied we're away, stalks off. He is the man in the photographs. Sniffing the air. Scanning the reeds. Testing the water with successive casts. An expert.

Four trout later, Philip tells us of his enthusiasm for the hunt. How he tossed in the job in the city, bought his place in the country, gave away the lot to indulge his sport. Of how he sometimes guides all day and then when he has shared his secrets and the guests are gone, fishes some more.

As do his previous books, *Trout n' About* and *The River Behind the Hill*, *Call of the River* brims with good talk and engaging stories. It is not the same as going fishing with Philip, but it is close. Now we have tales of New Zealand and even one of Europe to add to those of more familiar places; tales that cause a little tingle in the hairs on the back of the neck and make me think, I want it to be like this.

Philip's words are tales of passion. Yes, there are tips for the angler, directions to favourite waters, and hints of flies

Foreword

and feeding patterns. But through it all shines a love of what he does, not only of fish remembered but the whole experience of fly-fishing. There's no artifice here, just genuine affection. Philip Weigall's words warmly reflect the man himself, a man who simply loves to fish.

Steve Vizard

Contents

FOREWORD *iv*
1   THE HIGH SNOWYS   *1*
2   THE COOLER MONTHS   *17*
3   GUM BEETLES   *25*
4   THE SWAMP HARRIER   *39*
5   LAND OF THE LONG BROWN TROUT   *49*
6   THE BACKCOUNTRY   *61*
7   THE EVENING RISE   *75*
8   EUCUMBENE   *97*
9   SEASON'S END   *109*
10   JANE'S FISH   *125*
11   MIDGES   *135*
12   MACKENZIE COUNTRY   *149*
13   LOCAL LORE   *165*
14   THE WEE LAKES   *179*
15   THE CREEK   *193*
16   EUROPE   *203*
GLOSSARY   *231*
ACKNOWLEDGMENTS   *232*

One

The High Snowys

YOU KNOW HOW it happens. Plans are made for a special trip away, involving a certain kind of fishing. Yet when you actually get there, your plans are sabotaged by unexpected conditions. So it turned out when Simon and I headed to Corryong for some late summer stream fishing, heads filled with thoughts of hoppers and mayfly along pasture-lined valley streams.

It was not to be. Our visit coincided with the worst heatwave of the season. On the first afternoon, a thermometer reading from the Indi River confirmed our fears: 25 degrees. Right then, our plans for the valley streams were dashed.

The High Snowys

Now February on the upper Murray system can be great, but any visitor must be prepared for the possibility of the year's fiercest temperatures. With 2000-metre mountains looming nearby, it is easy to forget that the valleys themselves lie only a few hundred metres above sea level. The cool of a high country summer is an illusion here. Beneath these peaks, Victoria's highest daily temperature is usually recorded once or twice a year. Though the valley streams descend rapidly from higher elevations, and race along shaded courses, that is not enough protection from 40-degree heat. And once water temperatures rise into the mid-20s, trout fishing becomes a forlorn proposition.

But all is not lost in the Corryong district when the late summer heatwaves strike. Though we hadn't planned for it, there was a backup option. The mountains that shadow the upper Murray to the north and west are ramparts of a vast plateau. This isn't a table-flat plateau, but rather a table on top of which are hills, valleys, the odd ravine and the occasional true peak that justifies the term 'mountain'.

The broad name given to this vast, elevated area is the Snowy Mountains. Most of south-eastern Australia's greatest rivers are born here, at least in part: the Murray, the Murrumbidgee, the mighty Tumut, and the once-great Snowy itself. The Snowy Mountains are like an 'island in the sky', and the island in this case is laced with creeks and streams that will eventually unite to form these large rivers. On the plateau, few of the streams reach any size, but there are many elements that favour them as trout waters.

To begin with, they are about as natural as it is possible for a stream to be. Above 1300 metres, most are free from the dams and diversions of the giant Snowy Mountains Hydro-Electric Scheme. These waters are also largely shielded from civilisation's little curses like erosion and pollution, due to the protection offered by the massive Kosciuszko National Park.

Many of these headwater streams cannot be reached by road. The few four-wheel drive tracks that penetrate the wilderness are closed to all but emergency vehicles, so it's walking or nothing. The hike *in* is usually reasonable; mostly you travel along fairly level ridge lines, and then descend steeply into the river valley. A case of 'jelly legs' at the bottom of the sharpest pitches is the main discomfort suffered.

However, as you drop several hundred metres in little more than a kilometre, it pays not to spoil the day by dwelling on the walk *out*. Herein lies the catch to backpack angling in the Snowys: at the end of your adventure, when your feet are already sore and your legs tired from traversing a slippery, rubble-lined stream, the mountainside you must ascend looms like a vengeful god. You've had your fun in paradise, now pay the price.

Eventually, your burning knees, blistered feet and gasping lungs deliver you back to the car, which you've never been so glad to see. You drop to the ground swigging the half-bottle of lukewarm, flat Coke you left on the back seat as if it were the elixir of life. And then you vow *never* to fish that stream again. So what if the fishing was great? Nothing's worth a walk like that.

But the mind works in strange ways, and after an hour in an airconditioned car and a whole bottle of icy lemonade from the milk bar in Corryong, the memory of the walk out is already being swamped by happier thoughts. You see that magic drift when the Humpy quietly floated *under* the bank and out of sight, so that you struck into the invisible 2-pounder on the strength of faint ripple and a hunch. The endless sweep of bends on the snowgrass plain so rich in prime trout water that every square metre deserved a cast (and was often rewarded). Caddis fly appearing like snow flurries as soon as the sun broke from behind the cloud bank, or the distant thunderhead building in cook's hat whiteness behind the dark and craggy bulk of Mount Jagungal.

These are the thoughts that dominate, and they gently push the memory of the painful climb away. By Wodonga, you're already consulting the Natmap, looking for ways into the gorge further upstream for next year's trip.

Simon and I decided on our destination in the Snowys by first ruling out any water less than 1300 metres above sea level. As we pored over maps in the cabin on Wednesday evening the clock neared midnight, yet a mini-bombardment of beetles and moths against the flywire emphasised the muggy warmth outside. In the valleys, the night temperature would not drop far enough for long enough to cool our regular streams. The need to travel to high elevation on Thursday was reinforced.

The water we chose perfectly fitted the profile we had devised – at least on paper. The whole section we planned to hike into exceeded 1300 metres, yet we would strike the stream below the junction of several tributaries, where it should be of reasonable size. As a bonus, there appeared to be a track of sorts into the valley, which would negate the need for bush-bashing (at least on the way in). There was no meaningful mention of the stream in our various reference books, and I had to cast my mind back to old reports from acquaintances – and even older manuscripts – to grasp any idea of what to expect. This was a forgotten trout water, one whose memory had faded with the closing of tracks, and the creation of the 'glamour' Snowy waters: the huge lakes and the mighty tailwaters.

I was sure I had heard or read at least one reference to good-sized fish in our chosen stream, but this contradicted the usual situation of small trout in the high country creeks. Snowed in for five months of the year, and subjected to many frosts for the remainder, streams above the 1300-metre mark are usually not fertile enough to grow trout of any size. Only migration to or from a sizeable lake is likely to provide larger fish. Here, dams and diversions a long way downstream apparently ruled out any such migration.

While we hoped to strike an undiscovered vein of monster trout, our main objective was cool water, cool air, and plenty of willing takers of the dry fly. If they turned out to be half-pounders, that was fine. And the scenery was sure to be gorgeous.

Thursday found us revelling in the cool morning air at nearly 1800 metres. The bushfire wind that had brought a total fire ban day to all of Victoria and southern New South Wales was reduced to a pleasant breeze that kept the march flies away. The start of the track was where the map indicated, and at first the walk promised to be much less arduous than we feared. The surface was sandy rather than rocky, and the snow gum forest cast a mottled shade. The descent was noticeable but gradual, and within half an hour we could make out the river valley that was our destination.

Then the track abruptly veered left and everything changed. At once we were staggering down a steep slope, washed out with ankle-twisting runnels and covered in crumbling granite. Now that we were truly descending into the valley itself, the bottom seemed far away. We had already dropped a few hundred metres when a small clearing gave us our first glimpse of the stream – a silver line, way down below. The climb out would not be fun.

The clearing also suggested a particular spur line as the best route to the river: a well-timed discovery, as by now our 'track' was veering away from the course we wished to take. The spur turned out to be a good choice, and eventually we burst out of the inverted tree line onto soft snowgrass and low heath. The last few hundred metres to the creek passed close by some dizzy drops and led to one cliff-top dead end, but then we crested a small mound, and we were beside the stream.

Its size was as we expected: 3 to 5 metres wide, and

flowing impressively for a dry February. A quick temperature check showed the water to be 15 degrees – 10 degrees less than some of the lowland streams. Our first objective had been achieved.

I left Simon to start fishing right there, and chose to cut some bends downstream for a few hundred metres. The little river couldn't have looked prettier. Its long shallow runs were alpine clear, and at first glance appeared to offer no cover for the trout. A closer look revealed dark slots in the bedrock, and generous undercuts along the banks. The pools were surprisingly deep. I guessed the water clarity to offer nearly 3-metre visibility, but there were places where the stream bed was as vague as a shadow at night. Passage along the banks was unhindered by trees or scrub, and every footfall was cushioned by the soft snowgrass, sphagnum, or ankle-tall heath. This last plant looked wiry and ragged, as if it might trip a lazy step or claw at bare legs. Instead it was strangely frail, and caressed the skin like a hairbrush.

I was completely recharged by the time a particularly beguiling pool would let me travel no further. I began fishing a Royal Wulff, anticipating at once the quiet roll of a confident brown, or the over-excited slash of a rainbow. I did not expect large fish, but perhaps some honest pounders would be found among the more likely handspan-size specimens. And who was to say that a particularly adept fish, one that had learned to make the most of what opportunities there were at such an altitude, might not have grown to a couple of pounds?

Nothing came to the Wulff in that pool, nor in the run and pool after. I changed to a nymph for a while, then to a Geehi Beetle, then back to the Wulff again. The stream wound on, as perfect as ever, but by the time I caught up with Simon, I had not seen a single fish. At least my companion was able to report sighting two small trout, so the water wasn't entirely barren. Such was my dissatisfaction though, that the first thoughts of abandoning the stream began to creep in. The climb out would be rotten after so little time in the valley, but on the other hand, there was still time to travel to another better-known water, and grab a few hours of more predictable fishing before nightfall.

I didn't mention my musings to Simon, far less act on them. I felt a twinge of guilt for even considering giving up. We had spent scarcely half an hour on an unknown stream, and one that had taken considerable effort and planning to reach. 'How about some perseverance?' I told myself. But I couldn't entirely shake the misgivings. This was not a large, swirling, secretive river that could hide a dozen trout every 10 metres. Surely if the little stream held a respectable population of fish, we would have encountered more than two?

I worried for nothing because, slowly, we started to find more trout. For no apparent reason, fish began to appear in at least some of the places where they should have been. Then at last the Wulff was gone in a swirl. I was too out of tune to strike properly, and I never connected. Three casts later, the fly was snapped down to a more alert response, and I caught a foot-long rainbow. It wasn't as if the stream's appearance changed for the better, in fact it could be argued that the number of decent pools reduced, and the banks became less steep. Yet we were now fishing, instead of just hoping.

By early afternoon, the day was already nestling into a permanent place in my memory. The sky remained a deep, cool blue, and it was hard to imagine that the gentle breeze brushing our brows was fuelling forest fires less than a hundred kilometres away.

Up ahead, the valley formed a U-shape as if carved by glaciers, and the total lack of trees on the valley floor spoke of the intense winter frosts. Occasionally, we stumbled upon a strand of rusty wire or a weathered fence post: reminders of a cattle-grazing history, long gone. With effort, I drew my mind away from the serene valley before me, and to a recollected black-and-white photograph, taken near here half a century ago: two stockmen on horseback, pushing a dozen or so wide-eyed cattle through chest-deep snow. The caption was something like 'Caught by the Blizzard'.

I looked hard through the summer daisies and lazy mountain grasshoppers, and imagined this same scene in July. The north-south alignment of the valley would mean only a few hours of direct sunlight, and then only on the days between the snowstorms. Most green would be gone from the vegetation. Those patches blown free of snow or dug up by starving wild horses would be a watery straw colour. The stream itself would be lined with shards of ice, and during the worst frosts, when the night sky crackled clear in the wake of an Antarctic blast, the ice would grow across the stream to meet in a ghostly bridge. If snow followed soon after, the stream and its trout would vanish altogether for days on end.

I looked up again to the caddis dancing on the sun-bright water, and saw a fingerling leap for one. The little river and the valley looked so alive and fertile, but the scene was transitory. I could walk from this valley in hours, and drive back to the lowlands. Long before the first snowfall of autumn I would be gone. But the trout would stay. However endless the winter, however harsh, they had to survive it. The valley as I saw it probably existed for no more than a score of days a year.

I returned to my fishing, and with each half-pound trout I landed, there was a new sense of admiration. These fish were alpine survivors that could not be simply measured on the ruler alongside their cousins from the benign lowland streams.

Then, as my Wulff floated down a slightly deeper channel in a broad and shallow run, a dark shape gave chase and, in that thrilling way of such fish, ran the fly down, gulped it so I faced its jaws, and then turned upstream. Having practised on some lesser fish, I was able to pause for the turn before striking, and soon I had the trout of the day in the shallows at my feet. What a mountain fish! Nearly two pounds of brown trout – not a gaunt, desperate cannibal, but broad and deep. It was difficult to imagine how this fish could come from such a stream. Simon appeared around the downstream bend just after I released it, and there was a vague sense of regret that I hadn't been able to show him my prize. Still, the day had been kind to us both, and he had the generosity not to show the slightest doubt when I told my story.

The day became more relaxed with each fish caught. I suppose at some point we achieved whatever result it was that constituted success. The tally was not outstanding, and only that one trout was large enough to rate a special mention. Yet the high valley was beautiful, the water a pleasure to fish. The spectre of mountain weather was today no more than a benign and carefree presence. Even with the hard walk out, we would be able to say, 'Well that was definitely worth it.'

I always look forward to the point on a trip when the hard edge of badly wanting fish eases off. The whole package can then be appreciated: the wildlife, the setting, and the company. Around early afternoon, Simon and I took turns to sit back and eat lunch while the other fished, hungrier for a sun-warmed and slightly soggy sandwich than to see what lay around the next bend.

The route out was left further and further behind with every kilometre of stream, and by midafternoon I considered that perhaps it was time to turn back. The little river was shrinking with every tributary we passed, and while the fishing wasn't any worse than it had been, there seemed little chance of finding a hidden El Dorado. Simon was keener to persist. 'Let's give it another half hour,' he suggested. 'That'll still give us time to walk out and drive to another river for the evening rise if we want to.'

And so we continued. We had been leapfrogging most of the day, but by chance Simon caught up with me just as I spotted the most trout-shaped rock I had seen in ages. Two riffles, separated by a granite bar, spilled from the dark pool above, and the shape was sitting bang in the middle of the left-hand one. Had we been fishing a lowland stream, the shape could possibly have been a big carp, but there were no fish so large to be found in this little stream at 1500 metres. I pointed out the rock to Simon, joking that if it were a trout, I would probably faint on the spot! The blurred waters of the riffle were worth a cast, anyway, so I nonchalantly flicked the Wulff up into the current in the hope that an unseen fish would materialise from beside the shadow of the rock and grab the fly. But no. As the white wings bobbed past the rock, the whole thing glided to the right. I didn't faint, but my legs shook as I dropped to a stunned crouch. 'The bloody thing *is* a trout!' I whispered to myself as much as Simon.

Except for migrating lake spawners, I had seen few mountain stream trout as large, or more particularly, so solidly built. Though the monster trout had refused the Wulff, it seemed unfazed, and had drifted back to its station. The sun disappeared behind a lonely cloud, and I lost sight of the fish. I wasn't going to cast blind to a beauty like that, so I used the enforced halt in proceedings to change back again to that favourite alpine pattern, a Geehi Beetle. Perhaps the trout might have taken the Wulff next cast: I've known many fish to refuse a fly first time, then take it quite happily on a subsequent occasion. One ornery old New Zealand brown all but ignored an Adams ten times before taking it on the eleventh cast as if he'd seen it for the first time. All day the Wulff had worked well on the little stream. Was a change to the Geehi a considered tactic, or a panic response?

The shadow of the cloud raced away up the valley, driven by winds much stronger than those by the stream. There was the trout again, its position unchanged. From my distorted tail-end perspective, the fish looked impossibly broad. I could just make out the gentle sway of its body as it effortlessly held position against the current. On some level, I understood that I could not afford to fret and plot about this fish. Over-cautiousness would be more dangerous than action. The first cast had to be *the* cast, so I let it proceed without second thoughts.

Though it sounds melodramatic, from the point of that cast onward, I experienced a disembodied perspective. It was as if my conscious and analytical mind was pushed to one side, while my brain decided that it was best to let instinct take over. The fly alighted a forearm's length above and to the right of the trout's head. This brought not the slightest flicker of recognition from the great fish, but then as the current carried the Geehi Beetle directly alongside, it turned deliberately towards it and with one sideways stroke, stuck half its head out, engulfed the fly, then swung back upstream. All my life I have been cursed with the affliction of striking too soon, especially on large fish that I can see before they actually take the fly. This time, when it mattered as much as ever, I did not lift the rod until the trout faced upstream again. I knew it was hooked well before the sweep of the rod was completed.

The next few minutes were chaotic. The fish tried desperately to run up into the pool above, a pool that was clearly its home. I tried just as desperately to stop it. The upstream haven was lined with deeply undercut banks, littered with heath roots and driftwood. I am certain that if the trout had made the pool it would have broken me off. The struggle was close and fierce. The fish made two shattering jumps, and performed endless crocodile rolls. When its upstream sorties were thwarted, it lunged with equal violence for the rapids downstream. Finally it circled me, seemingly beaten but never lifting its head.

The trout was a brown, even larger than it had seemed at first. As I had guessed earlier, its weight was not so much in its length, but its girth – an extraordinary situation for an out-sized trout in a high-altitude stream. We had no scales and the weigh-net had been left back at the car as unnecessary baggage, so you can decide for yourself how big the trout was. Well before I first touched the fish, my concern changed from landing it successfully to liberating it safely. In terms of size for habitat, it was the most magnificent trout I had seen in all my fishing life, and I wanted it to survive. As if sensing this, the fish gave up its angry circling, and allowed me to gently cradle it without protest while it was still in the water. I'm pleased to say the trout never touched dry land.

I lifted it briefly for a rushed photograph – the last frame on the film – then removed the fly. Simon swayed it back and forth while I pulled the rod and line out of the way. The trout swam a few metres, then sulked in the very run from which it had been caught. It made a half-hearted attempt to breach the lip of the pool, but moved sideways at the last moment, as if confused about the route. Sensing the trout's intention, Simon pushed it gently by the tail up into the pool. It hung near the surface for a moment – an incongruous shape suspended in the air-like clarity of the water. Then it glided down into the depths, and disappeared among the shadows of the bank.

Two

The Cooler Months

THERE IS AN old joke that closed seasons exist more to protect anglers from themselves than to protect the trout. Some winter days, when the wind shrieks in from the north, and even thick woollen mittens are not enough to stop your fingers aching from the cold, it seems this might be more than just a comic line.

In many places closed seasons are imposed on trout streams – usually over winter – to protect spawning trout and their offspring from angler interference. I am an advocate of the stream closed season, and aside from trout management considerations, I rarely bothered with winter stream fishing even when and where it used to be allowed. It was so dreary.

The closure that applies to streams is less commonly found on lakes, however, the reasonable assumption being that a trout in a lake is not spawning, and that anglers wading still waters will not damage the eggs and fry hidden in the gravel. The result is that while confirmed stream fishers are protected from themselves by a closed season that corresponds with the worst time of year, those who also enjoy lake fishing are never free from the temptation. The lake fisher is further confused by the possibility – albeit a slender one – of finding a patch of very good fishing in winter.

My life-long friend David Julian never got the fishing bug as badly as me, choosing instead to lead an upstanding and fairly normal life. We had quite similar backgrounds, including the good fortune of having fathers who not only enjoyed fishing and enjoyed taking their children fishing, but who were (and are) close friends in their own right. How wonderful is every memory of those childhood trips away with David and his brother Peter, their father John, my own dad, and sometimes my younger brothers Derek and Mark as well. We fished all over Victoria: in the surf at Peterborough and the estuaries of the west coast. We cast flies, lure and bait to trout in the Otway streams, and to those in the Howqua near Sheepyard Flat.

A few decades on, David still enjoys fishing, especially fly-fishing for trout, but he wants there to be a fair chance of success or, at least, sport. I know that using 'sport' in this context has a ring to it that harks back to fox hunts and private English streams. Yet if my friends and I use the word, we know exactly what is meant. If Peter tells us that 'I didn't land any, but we had plenty of sport', we don't find it at all contradictory. He's saying that he saw lots of fish, had a number of chances, but in the end, through bad luck or sheer difficulty, no fish were landed. In our circle, someone who has had stacks of sport but no fish is often regarded as more fortunate than an angler with a trout or two on an otherwise featureless day.

And that's why it can be difficult to get David out for some winter fishing: not so much because the fish are hard to catch, but because of the lack of sport. It has become something of an obsession of mine to prove otherwise to him, but I have to say that I haven't made much progress. Every year I'm on the phone to David after my first successful (or at least promising) winter session. I'm smart enough not to actually blurt promises down the phone. Instead I talk about other things, and wait for David to ask about the fishing. He's almost certain to do this because he's an angler, and if not a fanatic he still wants to know. And given that I'm pretty much employed by things angling related, asking, 'How's the fishing?' is not so different from asking, 'How are you?'

If I'm patient, he will eventually enquire about the trout, and I'm ready. The trick to trying to round up company for winter fishing is to sound as if you don't actually care whether you have it to yourself or not. I'll tell David about the fish that have been caught (there are always a few, even in winter) and delete reference to the fishless trips. Hopefully, I'll also be able to drop a casual remark or two about the size of the trout. This is lake fishing we're talking about, and if any fish at all have been landed, they were probably of a fair size.

If I read David correctly, this is the moment when he usually wavers. 'How big did you say?' queries my friend, with the first sparks of enthusiasm. 'Well, the one I landed was a 6-pound brown,' I reply. 'But the one I missed on the strike swam over the same bare patch in the weed, and would have been at least 4 inches longer. So how are Katie and the kids?' 'Yeah fine,' he mutters distractedly. 'What were these trout taking?'

I've got him. David's highly developed sense of comfort can usually be relied upon to keep him safely away from the icy winds and persistent sogginess of a highland winter, but he has this thing about big trout. 'Don't we all?' I hear you say. Yes, however with David the itch to land a big one – and I think the old ten pounds might be the unspoken goal – is especially strong. I have seen him show uncharacteristic fortitude in the face of the elements when the smell of big trout is thick on the water.

'Well, I suppose it is time for my token winter fishing trip,' he announces. We arrange to meet at my place on Saturday at 10 am (David likes early starts even less than I do). Before I hang up, I remind him to bring plenty of 8-pound tippet. I believe salesmen call that a closure.

Call of the River

Hepburn Lagoon, near my central Victorian home, is one fishery that I've tried my best to lure David to during winter, with occasional success. Hepburn isn't merely regarded as good for winter fishing, but for being at its peak under miserable conditions. Even the Fisheries Department handbook, not renowned for straying far from the basic facts, allows that the lake 'reputedly fishes best in wet, cold weather'. Sure enough, some of my best days, in terms of large fish at least, have been the bleakest.

Hepburn vies with Lake Modewarre and Tasmania's near Western Lakes for being the most exposed, barren-looking water in Australia. Trees are scarce, and only the rounded hill on the north shore offers modest shelter. It's one of those lakes that actually leaves you feeling sorry for the wildlife on the bitterest days. Maybe the swans, ducks and moorhens have adapted to the winter gales, but they certainly look miserable as they bob lifelessly on the grey waves.

Only the trout seem impervious to the cold. True, when the water temperature moves south from about 5 degrees, even they become fairly inactive. Above this mark though, you can expect action. Not reliably of course – this is fly-fishing, on a lake, in winter. Yet on many days when I've run out of warm, dry places among my clothes to thaw aching fingers, the sudden crash of a fish to my painfully retrieved Tom Jones is followed by an instant electric run. The trout, at least, seem to be as vibrant as if it were a balmy spring day.

Despite the promise of a large fish, few anglers of any persuasion spend much time at Hepburn on the harsher winter days. For those who are out there, the usual short conversations-in-passing are tinged with a little more respect than chats during finer weather. There is a sense, unspoken, that we're the *serious* fishers, for whom the risk of flu and premature loss of circulation is reasonable if the big ones are about.

One such elderly fly-fisher I encountered several times over the seasons. Our meetings were random and well spaced – sometimes separated by years rather than months. We never exchanged names, only spare comments about the conditions and the fishing. Mostly I found him in the dead of winter, and on the really terrible days. Rain dripped off his crumpled felt hat and trickled down his nose, while the large knee-length oilskin that draped his thin frame was buffeted by the wind.

In the course of our shared days on Hepburn, I saw him land two fish under these conditions, both large male browns of 5 or 6 pounds that he fought to submission with slow experience. No doubt there were many more successes I wasn't around to see. But of course there were a lot of casts when nothing pulled on the line but the drifting strapweed and the sloshing waves. He didn't seem to mind. 'The big ones move better here during the cooler months,' he would say, 'and fewer fishing for 'em.' I never heard him utter the words 'winter' or 'cold'. Just 'the cooler months', as if this were a climatically pleasant period when compared to the heat of the other seasons.

Try as I might, I haven't had a lot of success converting David to the school that regards bleak as best. Our few winter trips together to Hepburn have dropped out of our personal angling folklore. Either they failed under blue skies, or else my friend's patience was too quickly exhausted in the face of highland winter squalls. If I mention the word 'Hepburn' in conversations, I'm likely to get a blank stare from David, followed perhaps by a look of faintly recalled discomfort, as if he's just bitten into a lemon pip.

I remember the one chance I had to turn David around, to show him why I bothered with the lake at all. On that winter day, I had misjudged the wind direction, thinking it to be southerly, and had chosen to approach the lake from the dairy end (which most quickly accesses the southern shore). On rounding the headland concealing my favourite bays, however, a stiff westerly laced with the obligatory sleety showers greeted us. Casting was possible, but it turned out that drifting strapweed stole the effectiveness of every second retrieve. When I cheerfully announced that the outlet shore (more than a kilometre away) might be a better bet, David murmured something about the best spots always being furthest from the bloody car, and trudged off in the suggested direction.

I took a minute to free some weed from the runners, and then cast the loose line out so as to reel it cleanly back onto the spool. Three turns and the handle was jerked from my wet fingers. My startled recovery clasped the line to the cork, and I was allowed a snapshot of relief as I felt the rod lurch under the load of a large trout. A moment later a huge, dark back breached among the weed several metres out, and I recovered my voice to shout 'Got one!' towards the departing figure, now a good hundred metres further west, head down and hood up against the wind. I looked back to the fish, which lunged down and up again to thrash the water . . . and then nothing.

It is always the same for me in those moments after a good fish has been lost. A few seconds of childlike denial that the trout has actually gone, as if wanting that big brown or rainbow badly enough will cause it to miraculously reattach to the line. And then the reality hits, and you're left standing there looking vaguely pathetic. Limp rod and line, flat water unmarked by fish, yet heart still pounding, breath still racing.

The seasoned angler is meant to take such a loss well, perhaps dipping his hat slightly in salute to the trout, and chuckling wryly about their next meeting. By midsummer, with several good fish safely landed for the season, I can almost manage this generous attitude to a beauty lost. In midwinter, wet and alone on Hepburn Lagoon, I felt crushed. David was even further away, evidently oblivious to the whole drama. I would tell my friend what had happened, but the moment was gone. He would politely feign interest, but to him I knew that the lost trout would merely join a long list of others he had never seen, never felt on his line. David hasn't visited Hepburn since.

Three

Gum Beetles

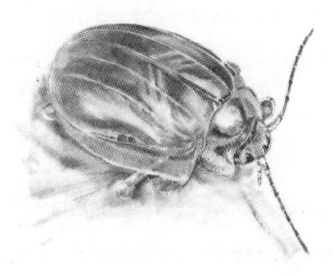

THE WAY THINGS worked out, Lindsay and Terry arrived in Tasmania three days before Ian and I could get there. This gave the brothers an enviable head start, which predictably I heard about soon enough.

Lindsay and I have fished together ever since a chance encounter on Victoria's Jim Crow Creek in the 1980s. Over the years, he's proven to be not only a very good fly-fisher, but also an enthusiastic and resilient one. On a day out with Lindsay, I'm always careful to stock up on muesli bars and portable drinks, because if the fishing shows any promise at all, we won't be heading back for lunch. Dinner is likely to

Gum Beetles

be a late affair as well.

One of the traditions that has developed between us is the 'call from the field': a phone call made by the one who is out fishing to the one who is not. The call *maker* holds the clear advantage, being the person who has just enjoyed a session on the water, and who is probably heading back out there shortly. For the call *receiver*, the experience is likely to be bittersweet. Every angler likes a fishing story – especially a fresh one. And yet knowing that your mate is out there among them while you are trapped in the office . . .

Lindsay's call from Tasmania came through the Saturday night before our Monday flight down there. I heard the pips and immediately pictured my friend in the Bronte Park phone box. It would be a clear, starry spring evening, and probably a bit chilly out there on the edge of the silent paddocks. Yet I could tell it had been no chore for Lindsay to leave the snug cabin fireside to make this call. 'Well, you should have been here today!' he began gleefully. Over the next five minutes I heard all about the dawn midge action in the slicks at Bradys Lake and the afternoon spinner falls at Lake Binney. He was well into recounting the polaroiding at the Great Lake the previous day, when the coin supply mercifully ran out. I was left holding the handset, pleased the fishing for the forthcoming week sounded so promising, and yet knowing the next thirty-six hours were going to pass awfully slowly. I phoned Ian to repeat what Lindsay had just told me. Ian loves fly-fishing as much as I do, and has fewer chances to get on the water. A day and a half out from a holiday in Tasmania, it would not have been possible to wind him up any more than he was. Still, it was nice to share the burden.

The days and hours until the start of a fishing trip pass eventually, no matter how unlikely that might seem at times. After the customary sleepless night, our aircraft was boarded Monday morning, and in no time the tip of Wilsons Promontory, the mainland's southernmost tip, was disappearing under the left wing. The cabin crew barely had time to serve breakfast and we were descending again. The deceptively serene-looking corrugations of Bass Strait swells were replaced by the green patchwork and distant blue mountains of Tasmania, and then we were on the ground.

The road trip from Launceston Airport to Bronte Park is akin to a journey through the pages of an angler's guidebook. On a sunny November day, rich in the height of spring, we passed one famous water after another – the South Esk, Brumbys Creek, then up the mighty Western Tiers past Arthurs Lake, the Great Lake, Shannon Lagoon, Little Pine . . . The names flicked by like billboards lining the entrance to a holiday town, each beckoning for our business. Fly-fishers have been known to leave Launceston for Bronte and never get there. Travel past kilometres of the Great Lake's deep blue welcome, or see the swallows flitting over Little Pine's ripple, and you can understand why. But Ian and I had plans for the afternoon centred nearer to our Bronte Park base, so with some effort of will we continued on.

Gum Beetles

The cabin at Bronte bore evidence of a recent and hasty lunch, accompanied by a single terse line on a piece of paper towel: 'Gone polaroiding near Shack Shore of Bradys – back after dark'. We unpacked the car, had a hasty lunch ourselves, and gathered the fly gear together. With the midafternoon sunlight still strong, we headed for some polaroiding too, but off Bradys Lake's north-west shore.

And at last, we were *there*, walking through the clumps of wallaby grass and wattle down the short, steep slope from the road to the water. Ian angled to the right, I to the left, ensuring we both had plenty of untouched shore to patrol. A light breeze blew from the south, just enough to generate a gentle wave on our shore. The lake was typically clear – not quite the brilliant clarity of the Great Lake or St Clair, but a delight all the same. Were it not for the mottling effect of the rubble lake bed, I would have expected to polaroid trout well before reaching the water's edge. I started walking slowly east, towards the forested bulk of Bradys Sugarloaf, with another high and nameless forest ridge to my left.

The tree-covered hills surrounding Bradys Lake are not merely a backdrop to the fishing. They also contain the right eucalypts to support a weird little insect of some importance to trout anglers: the gum beetle. And sure enough, as I focused more closely on the water ahead, I began to notice the pea-sized blobs of yellow–green beetles scattered every few metres.

Gum beetles are one of those obscure insects hardly

known to anyone except fly-fishers – and in this case, foresters as well. Fly-fishers mostly love them because they can cause trout to rise long and hard, and usually they are easily imitated by a fly. However, to our frustration trout do ignore gum beetles sometimes, and for no apparent reason. More on this shortly.

Foresters loathe gum beetles because when populations boom, they can seriously denude trees and slow their growth. At times, whole forests are sprayed from the air to combat these little leaf munchers. An angling acquaintance once told me he rescues a few jars of beetles when he hears spraying is imminent, then liberates them back into the trees when the danger has past. This may not be great news for timber production, but it does show the attachment fly-fishers can feel for an insect that may cause trout to take a dry fly.

Walking the bank of Bradys, lightly jewelled by a wiggly line of gold–green specks a few metres offshore, I reflected on my own attitude towards gum beetles. I like them, but it is strange how erratically trout feed on them. Considering many Tasmanian lakes have very large and therefore competitive trout populations, it is surprising how often an easy meal of gum beetles goes begging. How vexing it can be to enjoy supreme sport on gum beetle feeders one day, then watch them drifting around unscathed the next.

As I followed the line of beetles drifting along Bradys' shore under a clear afternoon sky, there wasn't a rise to be seen. The angle of the sun was lower than ideal down on the water's edge, and by the time I polaroided the first trout, it

Gum Beetles

was too close to cast to. An untidy presentation at the departing shape with a plastic beetle pattern brought no response – not surprising, given that the fish had swum under several real ones in ignorance.

I have long held a theory that gum beetles don't taste great, thinking this may partly explain the contrary attitude of trout to them. Some years ago on Tasmania's Penstock Lagoon, I watched fish rising hard to both jassids (a black and red leaf hopper) and gum beetles off the Sapling Shore. The gum beetles outnumbered jassids ten to one on the water, and yet it was a jassid pattern that finally caught me two nice browns. And the stomach contents? Two to one in favour of jassids. Given a choice, the fish had worked hard to select jassids over beetles.

A while later I casually mentioned this episode and the shaky theory to friend Ian Ainslie, a Tasmanian well acquainted with gum beetles. I think he took slight offence at the implied criticism of an insect so dear to him. But a few months later, he phoned and said, 'You're right about gum beetles. My son ate one the other day, and it tasted awful – like gum leaves.' Before I had a chance to say, 'He did *what*?', Ian added, 'But mayfly duns don't taste like anything – very bland.'

Do gum beetles taste so bad that the trout sometimes find the bitter eucalypt flavour outweighs the calorie benefit? As I ambled further down the line of untouched Bradys gum beetles, the theory was looking good. And then, suddenly, there was a rise. Fifty metres down the shore, the subtle 'snip' sound and rings were unmistakable. There it was again, a little nearer. Slow moving and close to shore, probably a brown. My musings ceased as I dropped to one knee and flicked a fly into the parade of naturals.

Too low to the water to polaroid effectively, I had to rely upon surface movement to track what seemed to be a single fish. As the rings came nearer, I noticed some gum beetles were missed, while other rises were for objects too small or drab to identify. This trout was eating gum beetles, but it wasn't desperate for them. Then a real beetle, 3 metres ahead of mine, vanished in a quiet suck. Seconds passed, my fly still there, ignored . . . must have swum on by now . . . sip . . . heck, that's mine, lift, he's on!

After a brief head shake of surprise, the brown trout shot straight out and down. Though it didn't look like an exceptional fish, I was taken aback by its strength – and grateful this stretch of shore lacked weed and snags. After a few minutes I worked the fish in quite close to the bank, only to have it zoom off again as soon as it was in sight. This it did repeatedly – seemingly beaten each time, and then kicking off again with renewed zeal. It took an effort to contain that early desperate edge to get the trip's first fish in hand, and instead show the required patience. But I managed it, and finally I had a fine brownie in hand. A solid 2 pounds, maybe a little more, and in hard highland condition. I yelled and waved at the speck in the distance that was Ian. Despite a faint wave back, I was unsure if my companion realised I'd caught a fish.

Gum Beetles

And so began a fine Tassie trip. It wasn't the most outstanding of my adventures over there, but it wasn't the toughest either. We caught fish every day we ventured out. Sometimes it was the four of us, dawn-patrolling Bronte tailers or the midge-slick feeders at Bradys; or hunting spinner feeders on light-wind afternoons among the logs at Lake Binney. Other times it was just Ian and me while the other two went elsewhere: polaroiding the shores of King William, Echo, Laughing Jack and Dee, or looking for rises and the odd tailer when cloudy skies robbed us of polaroiding light. Through the week, the gum beetles came and went, drawing a few rises from fish here and there, though more often ignored.

There were the usual victories and disappointments, hilarious post-mortems around the kitchen table late at night, and even a sense of mild competition when the brothers fished separately from Ian and me. I can remember all of it with great fondness. However one episode stands out with particular vividness.

It happened at Lake Binney. Binney is not a famous fly water. By Tasmanian standards, it would probably rank as 'average'. For much of the time, such a ranking would be a fair one, although it must be remembered that this is in the context of some of the finest trout lakes in the world. No, you won't find Binney featured in Tasmanian Tourist Bureau promotions, or even whispered about by clusters of worldly looking fly-fishers. But the lake does have its moments, and one of these was late in the last afternoon of our trip.

Earlier that same afternoon, a mild northerly and flat grey sky had brought the black spinners out along the north-east shore, and soon after, the trout had started jumping for them. Hunting these fish is exhilarating, if slightly perplexing. The slashes and leaps can appear totally random; and because a perfect presentation is crucial to success, finding the detail of a particular trout's beat is a must. Even then, choice of fly can be critical. Superficially, this seems simple – a Black Spinner pattern is the only contender. However, little things like sparseness of tie, hackle sheen and fly size sometimes seem to be of disproportionate importance. I've watched that great presentationist Rob Sloane furrow his brow in anxious search of his boxes for a spinner pattern with the right hackle tone.

For a while the spinner feeders kept us all entertained. I finally tricked one that periodically returned to the same little backwater, a pocket almost encircled by logs. After numerous casts, I eventually landed the fly in the right spot at the right moment, and in an instant a 3-pounder was attached and weaving out through the logs, with me hanging on desperately at the other end.

Half an hour later, the fun came to an end. A cold front that had threatened for hours finally marched in from the west. Instantly, the wind was in our faces, the temperature dropped, and the spinners were gone as if a spell had been cast. Over thermos coffee back at the car, new plans were formulated. Lindsay and Terry decided to head for Bronte Lagoon's Shack Shore to look for tailers under an increasingly gloomy sky. Ian and I chose to drive to the sheltered western side of Binney in the hope of finding a few relic spinner feeders.

While tall trees are found on all shores of Binney, many of those on the western shore are true giants. Though the tops of these gums waved and hissed in the gathering gale, the full force of the wind was broken at ground level. Only the occasional puff of breeze snuck through the forest defences to ruffle rain jackets as Ian and I proceeded down to the lakeside in search of trout. At first it seemed that spinners might yet be a chance in the lee of the forest barricade. But as 100 metres passed, then 200, not a spinner or a splashy rise did we see. Showery squalls seemed imminent, and perhaps that threat along with the gathering chill had sent the spinners to cover, despite the artificial calm.

The water was not entirely barren though. We began to notice the familiar green–gold blobs of gum beetles in the slick-calm water near the bank. 'Not being eaten of course,' said Ian, sounding annoyed. 'Just sitting there uselessly again.' He'd been unavoidably broken off by a big spinner feeder earlier, and I think he was feeling especially cheated by the recent wind change, having found another likely fish just before the front arrived.

I felt only slightly more optimistic about the gum beetle find. Nevertheless, I suggested we split up in case there were trout on the beetles somewhere. I cut inland, heading south towards a promontory about half a kilometre away, thus avoiding a slower walk along the awkwardly rocky and log-strewn bank. I left Ian to continue scanning the immediate shoreline.

A little later, I walked back out of the trees and onto the headland with renewed expectation. The wind was blowing along either flank of the point, and it was likely a concentrated slick of beetles and other flotsam would be forming off the tip. Sure enough, the slick was there, full of leaves and other rubbish, but also twitching insects – primarily gum beetles. I sat on a stump and watched, carefully scanning the trail for what might be tiny and easily missed rises. At length a fish did rise, twice, about 50 metres out. I stood up and false cast some line in preparation. Alas, no more rises followed.

I glanced casually back up the shore in Ian's direction, wondering what to do next, and beheld an interesting sight. In the middle distance was my friend, atop a giant fallen tree that sloped some 30 metres out into the lake before disappearing below the surface. Ian was at the very end of the tree, leaning forward and casting furiously. These old logs are bleached and slippery: not platforms you wander onto without good reason. There was no doubt Ian had found some action.

In a moment I had wound in and was jogging north as fast as I dared through the mess of rocks and tree litter. 'Out here, look!' Ian pointed as soon as I was within earshot. Gathering my breath, I stared offshore, and it took only seconds to spot the fish. Not just one or two, but perhaps a dozen. Porpoising, swirling, sickle tails and fins knifing through the water. Big fish, bigger than I had ever seen in Binney.

Briefly I wondered, Why here?, and then I noticed that the shore behind us was steeper and more thickly treed than elsewhere. No wind at all could blow through, so instead it blew over and around, only hitting the water 50 metres or more out in frustrated jabs. These bursts of wind actually swirled along and *towards* the shore, creating a giant eddy at least a hectare in size. This eddy seemed to gather and trap insects from the surrounding water. Even from a distance we could see hundreds of gum beetles, and this time the trout were eating them.

There was no hope at all of reaching the trout from the shore; only a precarious walk out on the polished, sloping wood of a long-fallen tree offered any chance. There was another such tree about 50 metres north of Ian, so I balanced my way out on it, trying to ignore the ever-increasing depth of water beneath with each slippery step. Close to the end, I found a knot that offered a modest foothold, and from there I commenced casting.

The trout were not as close as they seemed when viewed from the bank. Even casting the whole fly line, I was still short by a small but ruthless margin. The trout cruised about in happy ignorance of my gum-beetle pattern, which floated just a few metres inshore of them. Occasionally, a particular fish would start to work towards the edge of range, and then at the last moment quietly snip its way out again. Pleading with the fish not to turn away made no difference, and shouting abuse at them proved no help either. At such moments, you could almost swear the trout know how far you can cast, and hover just beyond.

The real reason was more clinical, but no less cruel. The cycle of wind bursts was such that the inshore swirls would push food towards us briefly, only to give in to periodic offshore blasts. In effect, the flotsam of insects and other debris was yo-yoing in front of us, while never quite drifting in over that crucial line.

And then it happened. What looked to be nearly an arm's length of razor-finned rainbow commenced its usual tantalising move towards me, then instead of turning away, it kept coming. For the barest moment I had my chance. I aerialised as much line as I could, hauled hard, and sent the line and its precious cargo rocketing towards the fish. I will tell you now it was a sweet cast, perhaps the best full fly-line cast I have ever done. Instead of the crash-landing, the line and leader laid out as gently as if I'd cast 13 metres, not 30.

For a dream-like instant, I saw the plastic gum beetle floating just ahead of the rainbow's last rise . . . and then it was gone in a gentle clip. I lifted the rod high and hard, simultaneously hauling with my left hand to help set the distant hook. And yes, the fish was there! A pale flash, then a boil way out in the lake to confirm the wonderful tension I felt through the rod and line. Down went the tip under the load of the best fish of the trip . . . and then sprang back up again. Slack line . . . what the? . . . desperately stripping in case the trout was still there, swimming straight at me. And

Gum Beetles

then the slow realisation that it's gone, the line tip and fly unceremoniously skating towards me. 'Ahhh . . . NO!' cried Ian from the next log, as if it were his own fish that had been lost. I shrugged silently.

I checked the hook, grateful in some remote part of my brain that the fly was still attached and the gape unopened. With effort I shook from the stupor of disappointment, and began scanning again for another fish. But something had changed. Perhaps it was a shift in the wind direction, or its strength. Whichever, the beetles and trout were moving slowly away like an empty life raft.

There was no point in staying out on the logs. Ian and I walked tiredly back to the safer ground of the shore. It wasn't so much that a big fish had been lost which bothered us. It was the failure to land a single trout when they were so *catchable*, but for a rod length or two of distance.

However, soon we were looking for fish again, renewed purpose in our step. This was Tasmania, and somewhere there would be other trout to catch. A solitary gum beetle buzzed unevenly across the open rocky ground between the trees and the lake, and landed on my shoulder. The beetles had not flown for hours: all those on the water were the residue of flights before the passage of the cold front. I casually pointed it out to Ian, and he said, 'Well, I don't know if that's a blessing or a curse.'

Four

The Swamp Harrier

IT ISN'T UNTIL October that spring really arrives around my home in the central Victorian highlands. September may throw in the odd day of sunshine and gentle wind, but if you watch the plants – and plants know about these things – you can see they aren't fooled. The young eucalypts in the upper paddock hold back their new shoots, the grass barely grows and the fruit trees hardly stir from their skeletal winter garb. On the lakes, a few damselflies and dragonflies bravely emerge, but you have to look hard to find one. By November they will smother the reeds in their thousands.

October is truly spring though. On Cabin Lake, part of

the Millbrook Lakes fishery and only a few minutes from home, it is the time when the waterfowl chicks become apparent as they join their parents for that first tentative paddle. On those days when jumpers and jackets can be shed without a second thought, the ducklings and cygnets are out there cheeping busily behind protective mums and dads.

But spring isn't all about plenty and security. Over the back of the hill behind Cabin Lake lies Shadow Lake, and in October 1999 the cygnets there almost died. Deceived by prolonged drought, the parent swans nested on an 'island' that is normally a reef, knee-deep under water. As the spring inflows filled Shadow, the reed nest was gradually inundated. Three days of violent storms racked the district at the worst moment, and when they subsided I arrived at the lake to find the nest washed away, the reed straws littering the north shore. But a miracle – in the far corner were the two swans, complete with a waterborne brood of six fluffy youngsters. Within a few days the swans even managed to rebuild a nest in a more sensible location, and all the cygnets were successfully reared by summer.

Meanwhile, a black duck family on Cabin Lake had enjoyed a profitable hatching, as could be seen by a line of about a dozen tiny ducklings that dutifully followed behind the patient squawkings of one or both parents. Occasionally, if you came upon the family unexpectedly and at close quarters, there would be momentary confusion: the angler briefly excited into thinking the hearty reed-side plops were rising trout, the ducklings scattering in fright. Within minutes, though, order would be restored. The fly-fisher would discover his mistake (with mild disappointment) and the ducks would identify the large, ungainly and upright animal on the bank as fairly harmless – at least on this water.

The best mayfly dun hatches begin to build at Millbrook in October, lasting well into December. There is a distinct association between the presence of baby waterfowl and some of the best fishing of the year, and so you'll find many fly-fishers barracking for the youngsters. At least subconsciously, we find ourselves wishing these little signs of spring well. And let's face it, baby birds are just plain cute. When the odds are overcome and the young birds survive the perils of those first few weeks (as with the cygnets at Shadow Lake), you find yourself offering a little cheer.

The various waterfowl and their young were out in force on Cabin Lake as I headed off to look for a dun hatch late that same October. After a lengthy morning deskbound, I had felt the need for some fresh air, and decided some mayfly research was required.

The conditions turned out to be ideal – mild with about two-thirds cloud cover – and I was soon racing around the shore trying to decide which trout to cast to. The duns hatched in pulses, as they usually do. And every time I chased one fish, a specimen a bit further up the bank seemed to start porpoising more regularly and closer to shore.

It took me about ten minutes to settle down and prop in

the south-west corner, where the emergence and the rise were as good as anywhere. With effort, I ignored the temptation of a big brown that sipped six duns off the top with methodical purpose about 50 metres along. I even refrained from covering the single slashing rise of a zooming rainbow right out in front of me. Only a matter of time, I told myself, before a fish starts to rise regularly and within range.

The hatch waned a little, and then a large grey cloud drifted over, bringing a slight chill to the air and a few drops of rain. At once the duns began popping again, and in the gloomy coolness they took much longer to dry their wings and fly to safety. Within a minute, dozens of tiny sailboards drifted around in my corner, and seconds later the first disappeared in the deliberate chomp of a large rainbow. Though it moved quickly, this was one of those trout the dun fisher hopes for. Every insect in its path was taken, provided it didn't have to deviate more than a handspan from its course. The cast had to be fast and accurate, yet the distance was short and the Barry Lodge emerger landed about a metre dead ahead of the trout. I barely had time to drop the rod tip, and the fly was gone. No need for much of a pause, just up with the rod and wwhhirrrrr – the rainbow was already heading for the far shore at full speed.

Large maiden rainbows are fish that invariably justify the effort to pursue them with fight alone. If you can also sight-fish, especially with a dry, then that's a bonus. Is there another freshwater sportfish that responds to the hook with such acceleration and power? Browns may slog it out with more cunning, chinook salmon with more long-distance endurance, but the sheer energy of a silver-green rainbow in its prime defies belief. It doesn't matter whether we're talking about the Great Lake, Eucumbene or Millbrook – these are magnificent, mighty fish

The rainbow was more than 6 pounds and easily could have buried me in the weed: at one point it was an awfully long way offshore, and a shallow dive would have snagged me. At such distance, there wasn't a thing I could have done to prevent it. Yet the trout chose to fight cleanly. I was able to use the release tool on the fish while it was still lively, and it shot away before I had a chance to offer a reviving hand.

After that, the fishing became more difficult. The emergence remained reasonable, but the behaviour of the trout veered towards unpredictable again. Individual fish began to change from duns, to emergers, to nymphs, and back to duns, without any clear reason or rhythm. It always niggles me when a feeding trout decides to swim straight under several perfectly helpless, juicy duns. And that is exactly what many fish on Cabin Lake began to do. I changed to a nymph, then to some very low-floating emergers, but it seemed that whatever I chose, the trout I was chasing decided to change its mind yet again. Finally, as the hatch started to fade at around 2 pm, some fish realised the error of their ways and made a last-minute bid for the disappearing duns. I covered one with a Highland Dun, and it took beautifully – a green-gold brown of a bit over 4 pounds. By the time I'd brought it in, the hatch was all but finished, so I headed back to the cabin verandah for a late lunch.

While I had fished, many of the waterbirds had been enjoying the mayfly feast in the background, along with the ever-present swallows. And with my blessing – there's plenty for all during a good emergence. As the hatch died, however, the background squawks, splashes and squabbles also diminished, and a definite post-feast quiet settled over the lake. I sat down for an overdue coffee and sandwich, and was soon joined by friend Trevor, who was guiding an American couple. Notes were compared, and it turned out that Trevor and company had enjoyed plenty of sport at Shadow Lake. Although his crew were fairly inexperienced, a 6-pounder had been landed successfully, and they had also encountered a few trout that were beyond their fish-playing skills. I recalled my rainbow and sympathised – big trout in their mid-spring prime are a handful for anyone, let alone novices.

Still, the Americans couldn't have been happier. Even one beauty during a dun hatch is a victory in itself. The husband was also a keen birdwatcher, and by chance Trevor was an expert on the subject. Trevor is a genuine expert on a lot of things. He's one of those rare people who follows up every interest with thorough research and at least a burst of involvement. If an eighteenth-century Polynesian wood-carving ever took his fancy, I'm sure he would buy three or four books on the subject, read them cover to cover, and then travel to the islands for a bit of first-hand investigation.

The abundant birdlife was a bonus for the visitors, and there was Trevor, able to name every species and discuss their habits.

We were just finishing our meals when another cacophony of bird calls sounded from the lake, but this time they carried a panicked edge. A glance across the water revealed the cause. A swamp harrier (a large hawk) had swooped from its hiding place among the copse on the far side, and was trying to grasp a small coot in its claws. I had watched harriers work before, and knew that their hunting strategy relied on surprise. Though this bird repeatedly swooped on the young dab-chicks and moorhens, the warning cries of others had bought precious seconds, and the alerted waterfowl were able to dive to comparative safety beneath the water weeds. It looked as if this particular raid would fail. Then the harrier spotted the ducklings.

Usually the black duck parents were careful never to take their brood far from the thick scrub overhanging two of the Cabin Lake islands. However, this time they were caught just off the third island, flanked only by tussocks and grass. Eighty metres of open water lay between the brood and the safety of the nearest willow thicket.

The tiny ducklings cheeped in a frightened bunch as the harrier climbed, then dived with talons outstretched. To our astonishment, however, just as the hawk was about to strike, the mother duck reared straight at it, squawking wildly with wings fully extended. Though the raptor was twice her size, it was thrown temporarily by this bravery, and its momentum was lost. The hawk climbed again, the duck taking the chance to frantically herd her babies towards the willows. They were less than halfway when the enraged hawk dived again, and this time a straggling duckling was surely doomed. Yet with the harrier's claws just inches from the little bird, the black duck hurled herself once again between the two in a shower of spray and wings, and again the hunter was defeated.

It seemed that the hawk gave up then, turning forlornly to the south and disappearing over the trees and out of sight. The mother duck guided her shaken brood towards the sanctuary of the overhanging willow branches. The first few little birds were soon safe beneath the willow when the harrier surprised us all by diving out of nowhere, hidden until the last moment by the island's tallest trees. Apparently we onlookers were invisible to the players, for by now the fight was within metres of the verandah from which we watched. Again the mother duck hurled herself at the huge hawk as it clawed with frustration at the branches beneath which the ducklings scurried one by one. At last the duck herself bolted in under the willow, her brood all safely beneath it. The harrier circled the island twice and disappeared.

It took a moment to take in what we had just witnessed. One of the most successful birds of prey had ambushed a dozen ducklings 80 metres from cover, with a solitary parent the only obstacle. Normally, I'm sure a swamp harrier could kill an adult black duck, but somehow this hawk seemed to be bluffed by the sheer courage and ferocity of a mother's defence.

There was a breathless quiet among us on the verandah. On one level, we wanted to cheer the black duck for her efforts, but we knew this would be crass. Perhaps the harrier had a chick in its nest that would be brought one step closer to starvation by the failure of the hunt.

Trevor told me once that he used to hunt ducks, but having witnessed a similar battle between a hawk and ducks on another lake some years ago, he no longer does. He's a hunter and a fisher by nature, as I am. But he has made his choice, and after seeing what happened that afternoon on Cabin Lake, I understand.

Five

Land of the Long Brown Trout

As far as I can tell from talking to visitors, Australia is underrated as a trout fishing destination. We have fine rivers and lakes, lots of good-sized trout, and, best of all, compared to many crowded northern hemisphere waters, we still have plenty of room.

An Australian fly-fisher might happily live his or her fishing life believing things couldn't be much better, but this illusion is spoiled by the fact that three aircraft hours east is New Zealand. By any objective standard, this country has the finest trout fishery on earth. Pick any criteria you like – climate, people, scenery, variety, lack of fishing pressure, quality of trout, sight fishing – and it wins. A friend who skied, once told me that Aspen had 'spoiled her for anywhere else'. ELAS she called it: exotic location addiction syndrome. She was only half joking. New Zealand holds the same threat to visiting fly-fishers.

To reinforce the dangers of this condition, I once made the mistake of taking an ELAS-afflicted acquaintance to my beloved north-east Victoria. Though a born-and-bred Australian, a family background that fairly swam in money had seen him do virtually all his fly-fishing in New Zealand. 'Look at that pod of fish working the duns!' I said to him as we stepped out of the car onto a high bank of the Kiewa River. There were several fish, the largest close to a pound-and-a-half, all rising beautifully. 'I don't really fish to anything under 4 pounds,' he yawned. I knew then it was going to be a long couple of days.

It was a strange pity, not envy, I felt for this bloke. We all like to catch a big trout, but how limiting would it be if *only* big trout sufficed? Think of all the small streams and alpine lakes crossed off the list. A visit to the land of the long brown trout needs to be regarded as a wonderful exception, not a benchmark.

Trout please me pretty much anywhere, and at any size. I don't think I am in too much danger of becoming a New Zealand junkie, even in the unlikely event that I suddenly find myself with a limitless supply of travel funds. But I do have, and always will have, an unashamed adoration for the place. When I first glimpse land out of the aircraft window a

Call of the River

few hours east of Melbourne Airport, I always feel the same as I do when beaching an unexpectedly large trout: excited and a little dazed all at once.

At the upper end of New Zealand's South Island, and an ice age or two ago, a massive glacier ground its way through a thousand metres of bedrock to form a classic U-shaped valley. The creaking wall of ice was twice the height of the tallest skyscrapers, and wider than Sydney Harbour Bridge. It travelled its bulldozing way for several kilometres before the global climate enjoyed a periodic warming. The glacier then began to retreat, leaving behind an untidy pile of rock to mark its turning point.

Today, Lake Rotoroa Lodge sits just to one side of this glacial moraine, though a bit of imagination is needed to locate it. The rubble is now clothed in smoothing vegetation, except for where the quietly turbulent Gowan River exits the lake that gives the lodge its name. The most beautiful legacy of the glacier is the lake itself, all but filling the lower valley. It runs due south from the lodge, over a kilometre wide and as many long. The peaks that shadow it climb more than 2000 metres above the water and are usually marked with snow. All shores are cloaked in forest right to the lake's edge, and the whole valley and beyond is preserved by national park. Just to make it all quite perfect, the lake is often glassy calm, reflecting the scene like a big green mirror.

I've never managed to arrive at the lodge with a clear head, and that is nothing to do with the complimentary drinks on the flight over. The same dazed feeling that I remarked on earlier persists, only now I think it is partly a function of all the trout water between Nelson Airport and the lodge. The car trip down crosses or follows several major rivers, some with names I recognise like the Moteuka, the mighty Buller, and then the Gowan itself. Others flash by – acquaintances met just once, the names familiar or the appearance of the water, but seldom both. Partly I want to stop the car, get out and have a cast. But partly I don't because I wouldn't know where to begin.

Upon arrival at the lodge, there's the owner Bob Haswell to greet me, all smiles and enthusiasm. Yes, the fishing's been good (it usually is) and he probably has a guest's story to prove it: so-and-so got eight yesterday, the best a 9-pounder. This is the sort of fishing report I like: not from last week, but less than twenty-four hours old. By the time the guests get in from the day's fishing, there will be even fresher stories, because barring some freakish weather event some fish will have been caught just hours ago, and big ones too.

I try to pay attention to Bob, which shouldn't be too hard given the subject matter, but my glance keeps flipping towards the Gowan River just at the back of the lawn. A trout rises, the powerful swaying rise of a fish you would pray for outside of this country. There's another. 'On the caddis,' says Bob, not at all offended by a fly-fisher's straying eyes. 'They've been on 'em most evenings this week.' This is said without great enthusiasm. Neither Bob nor his guides get terribly excited by the Gowan outlet, or the lake for that matter, although they allow that the river a kilometre or so downstream can fish reasonably. I silently think that if this bit of water were in Australia – the river outlet or the lake – you would need to join a queue to fish it. Yet here I am having a nice chat without so much as unpacking my fishing gear. This is what I mean when I talk about feeling a little disorientated.

I step inside, vowing that in a few minutes I will be out there casting to the caddis feeders. But there's Bob again, offering a cold beer. A fire burns in the lounge by the snug little bar. The late afternoon air isn't all that cool, yet the fire draws me closer. I look out through the huge window that frames the lake. Its waters are calm, as usual, and a pall of mist hangs over the centre – a legacy of a recent shower of rain. Being October, the high peaks that surround the lake are patched with snow.

The sun is starting to descend towards the tallest tops to the west, and I'm just finishing the beer, before grabbing my rod, when my friend Felix returns from his day's adventures. Felix arrived twenty-four hours earlier, and so he and Craig (our guide for the trip) already have a river or two to report on. I'm desperate to have a cast myself, but I also want to hear what they've done today. The Gowan can wait a few more minutes.

I've never seen anglers returning to the lodge downcast, however the level of outward enthusiasm does vary. There's the quietly pleased but slightly exhausted look of those who've managed a fish or two on a tough day (complete skunkings are almost unknown here). At the other end are those who've broken the magic '10', either in weight or numbers. Guides and fishers are likely to be equally wide-eyed and slightly nutty after such an event, talking loudly and a little too fast, and spending longer than usual at the bar.

Felix and Craig lean towards the latter state. They've obviously had a good day, and it transpires that Felix has landed seven trout, most around the 5-pound mark. I don't know whether to race out the door with my rod right then, or stay to hear the full account. I choose to stay, finally acknowledging to myself that the trout are safe from me this evening. It's odd, but having made the decision to leave the fishing for tomorrow, I feel myself settling in to the holiday. I take a chair and enjoy the whole recount of a great day's fishing. There is consolation in the knowledge that tomorrow I will be out on the rivers myself.

That seems to be how most of my New Zealand visits begin. This contrasts with regular trips, where a trout before bedtime on that first evening, or at least a cast, seems necessary to quell the fishing bug long enough to get some sleep. So why is it different in New Zealand, where the anticipation of the fishing to come should generate the worst insomnia?

On the trip in question, I once again defied expectations and slept soundly the first night. I awoke to the busy chatter of birds – normally a sign of fine weather. Some threat of rain had hung over the district the previous day, and I had drifted off to the sound of a passing shower. The morning view up the valley showed the clouds shredding by the minute, and early sunlight flickered on patches of hillside. The giant beech tree outside my window dripped solemnly, but sunbeams were already burning a soft steam off its boughs.

There was a controlled rush to the day's beginnings. Margaret the chef knocked on my door as she passed at 7 am (as requested) but I was well awake, the soundness of my sleep broken by the first hint of daylight through the curtains. In fact I was already showered and dressed, and using the extra time to pack for the day, weighing necessity against bulk. The camera and rainjacket in, vest in, hat in, jumper out, spare socks for the drive home . . . in.

Normally I'm not a morning person, preferring to be left to munch my way wordlessly through cereal and toast. On a fishing trip it's different, and at Lake Rotoroa Lodge I can be downright chatty. I can't match it with Bob though, who runs around as if he's been up for hours (and he'll have you believe that he has), bellowing good mornings in a tone that would be irritating anywhere else, but which is perfectly tolerable here. He dances back and forth, refilling coffee cups, prophesying about the fishing day ahead, indulging in some gentle ribbing, and solemnly offering his weather report.

It rains a lot at Lake Rotoroa, so weather is a popular topic. The rain and fishing are perfectly compatible, however most of us have a basically soft nature and would prefer to fish under sunny skies. Bob's reports supposedly come right from his secret source at the top of the New Zealand

Weather Bureau, so it's surprising that they're almost always in one of three forms: if it's fine, then it will stay fine; if it's raining, then it is due to clear up this morning; and if it looks like it's about to rain, then it's only a weak front that will pass through quickly.

On this particular morning, Bob went for forecast A, and he turned out to be right. By the time Craig, Felix and I pulled over in the paddock next to the appointed stream, the sunshine was unbroken. Our guide pronounced the water 'a bit murky' as it was slightly tannin stained after the overnight rain. Visibility was down to a couple of metres. I told Craig that in Australia, we don't often get water *clearer* than that.

We met the stream at an old ford. It was a creek by New Zealand standards, a few metres wide, fast and rocky and with a significant pool every hundred metres or so. Back home this would be a great little river for fast dry fly-fishing to pounders. Craig said that it contained no small fish, and that all the remainder would be found in the scattered pools – usually one fish per pool.

The pool at the ford was roughly circular on a tight bend, the force of the current pushing hard against the left bank, and a big frothy eye on the right. I was offered starting rights by Felix, who could afford to be generous after the previous day's successes. I fished a caddis grub pattern about half a metre beneath a greased wool indicator. The pattern was a beautifully ribbed masterpiece by fly-tier friend David Dodd. 'That's a fly I'd save for a special fish,' said Craig as he examined it. New Zealand guides love caddis patterns, and he was very impressed. 'The first fish of the trip *is* a special one,' I laughed, tying it on.

While Craig peered through the scrub trying to locate a trout among the morning shadow, I worked the pool as he instructed. First to the left, along the current line, then cautiously to the lower end of the eye. 'Here's one,' hissed Craig. 'Right in front of me, under the thickest patch of foam.' I cast automatically, perhaps recklessly, and landed the fly just above the white froth. A second passed, then, 'He's got it!' yelled Craig, and simultaneously the indicator twitched slightly. I lifted into a heavy, stubborn weight that I would certainly have picked as a snag on my own. The big brown didn't budge at first, but when it did it lunged for the top of the pool with great weight and power. I remember feeling at once overwhelmed and slightly ridiculous, playing a very large trout in a pool the size of a carport and no more than a metre deep. The upstream lunges worked in my favour, but they didn't last. Soon the trout was making for the downstream exit, and with a steep rapid lined with driftwood and willow below, I couldn't let that happen. Three times I turned the fish at the very lip of the rapid by applying all the sidestrain I dared. On the fourth lunge, the trout made it over the edge, but the momentum of my rod swung it in towards my bank, and it looked beaten and disorientated as it finned in a shallow pocket out of the main current.

Then there was a yank and a splash, and the fish was gone. The line had broken. I could have sworn that nowhere near enough pressure for a break-off had been applied in that instant, but things happen fast and unexpectedly where big trout are concerned. A weak knot, the line grazed on a sharp rock, or my own misjudgement? Ah well.

The stream continued to offer us similar chances. Sometimes we actually succeeded in landing a trout, sometimes the strike was missed, and of course the occasional fish refused our offerings altogether. Not many though. The trout seemed fired up by the mild spate, and were surprisingly aggressive takers, often moving a body length sideways to take the nymph.

Sharing such fishing is never a chore. Each brownie tackled is over 2-feet long, and after an encounter, successful or not, it is nice to stand back and catch your breath. Fishing with a partner also gives you a chance to look away from the river from time to time. In this district, the view is invariably breathtaking. While the valley floors often feature relatively flat and gentle topography, the surrounding slopes are the opposite. Neck-twisting bluffs and knife-edge ridges are everywhere. Trees cling to all but the highest and steepest slopes, though landslips gash the forest here and there as testimony to their precarious hold. Occasionally, the abrupt rise of an old fault line is encountered, marking where a whole chunk of countryside has simply risen a few metres. You are reminded that this is a young country, still growing up out of the sea.

After a late morning cup of thermos tea, we followed the creek down to its confluence with a larger stream, and there we spent the rest of the day. Initially the fishing was quiet, but by midafternoon the trout appeared again, and we landed a few more.

Usually we cease fishing around Lake Rotoroa when the light gets too low for effective polaroiding. This gets you off the water well before dark, and you may think this is too early. But the sport is sufficiently intense and demanding, so that even the obsessed are more than content to retire back to the lodge in time for a civilised dinner. Those caddis feeders are sure to be rising in the Gowan River twilight for the benefit of any diehards, but they are rarely pursued.

Felix and I had landed over half-a-dozen trout for the day, all around wrist-to-shoulder long, and as heavy as 7 pounds. We missed at least that many again. I had spent a single day in New Zealand and with more to come, I could not have been more content joining my companions and other guests at the bar, swapping stories of the day's events. The dazed sensation from twenty-four hours earlier was gone completely.

Six

The Backcountry

TIME PASSES TOO quickly on a fishing trip. Before I knew it, a few days at Lake Rotoroa Lodge had passed, and only a couple more lay ahead. Nevertheless, at the close of the third day I climbed into bed in a state of supreme contentment. By the glow of the bedside lamp, I unfurled a giant map of the northern South Island, and tried to make sense of our travels over the last day. This wasn't easy, because although guide Craig hadn't exactly blindfolded Felix and me, he hadn't carefully explained the landmarks either. There was that unmarked shortcut, and then travel on what appeared to be a private road. Whenever the name of a certain stream was requested, Craig's accent would thicken a couple of notches, and a several-syllable word would clatter out. Then before you could ask, 'The Toki *whatsa whatsit* River?', he'd distract you with something like, 'And just around that bend last week, I saw a nice brownie – would've been 9 pounds – feeding on big duns.'

Still, as I pored over the map, some familiar features appeared. Ah yes... there was the town of Murchison, where we had stopped for a cold drink. And a bit further on, the Buller River. *That* was one name I wouldn't forget after a childhood spent beneath a mountain of the same name. The 'Makamokarota'? Sounded familiar, or was it the 'Mikamakorata' we fished? With a yawn, I let the map slide to the floor, making a mental note to silently repeat any stream names Craig divulged the next day.

My sleep that night should have been unbroken, except that sometime around midnight, rain began to fall. The gentle drumming on the roof woke me more easily than a siren. Sometimes rain threatens fishing, sometimes it helps, but its effect is seldom neutral. I lay awake in the dark, listening and trying to judge how heavy it was. Light rain would probably help the fishing if it brought a small fresh to the rivers. However, this was New Zealand, and wherever you fish there are reminders of another consequence of rain: the savagery of mountain floods. Most of the rivers have their beds swept bare many metres from normal high-water mark, and wherever the flow is confined by gorges and cliffs, there is always a water-borne tree skeleton jammed into the rock so far above the river that it seems it must be the result of an elaborate hoax. Yet floods do that here, rearranging whole riverbeds so that entire pools disappear, only to re-form elsewhere. You hear stories of trout buried alive in the maelstrom, their battered tails protruding from the rubble once the water subsides. You also hear of the remarkable ability of the fish to ride out the floods, of trout seen finning quietly in the flooded rainforest several metres above their usual homes, while the whitewater tears at the valley just beyond.

The latter tale seems more likely. As quickly as they rise, the streams subside again. I have caught active and healthy trout in one river twenty-four hours after a flash flood reduced it to a washing machine with brown water.

Trying to hold the last image in my head, I drifted off again. I awoke at first light to silence. The rain had stopped. However, the dawn sky was thick and grey, with no hint of sunshine. At breakfast, the talk was about the rain and nothing else. A Sydney bond-dealer, English property developer, a Chicago dentist and Felix all compared notes with grave interest. Felix thought the rain had stopped around 1 am, but the dentist insisted it was still falling when he got up for a widdle at 4. Right on cue, Bob waltzed in with two plates of bacon and eggs. 'Just a passing shower,' he assured us. 'The forecast's for it to clear away completely this morning.'

The guides weren't so sure. As they huddled in earnest discussion I overheard snippets: 'About 4 inches at Ian's since yesterday . . .' 'The Owen's muddy at the bridge . . .' '. . . coming in heavier later this arvo . . .' Finally, Craig came over to our table. 'I'm thinking we might go for a bit of a walk today,' he suggested. 'What do you think?'

The walking track to our chosen stream skirted a lake hemmed by huge mountains, before turning up a tributary valley. It was raining again by the time we rounded a bend in the path and saw the river for the first time. For an instant my heart sank at the dirty grey colour of the stream. But then I realised it was the river *bed* I was seeing, through water so clear that only the barest tinge of aquamarine gave it away. 'Do we start here?' Felix asked hopefully, with me concurring silently. 'A bit further yet,' said Craig, and the track veered back into the forest once again.

Though I was eager to begin fishing, I couldn't avoid noticing the surroundings. For the first time I was in true New Zealand wilderness, completely inaccessible except on foot. Not even horses ventured into this heavily protected national park. The track was muddy in places, but wide and well formed. New Zealanders love their walking, or tramping as they call it. Perhaps they realised long ago that it was the only viable way of accessing much of the country. The attitude to a long walk is entirely positive. They don't view a hike into a fishing spot as an obstacle to be surmounted, but as an experience to be enjoyed in its own right. I should try thinking a bit more like that back home.

The path around the lake cut into a steep slope, but when

it followed the river the ground flattened out. We were once again in an old glacial valley, and while the mountains towering overhead were so steep they seemed about to topple over, along the river the grade was quite gentle. Periodically the track would break out into broad natural clearings, lush with grass. I thought I glimpsed a deer at the end of one. Eventually the path brushed the river again, and Craig announced it as our starting point.

By now, a steady drizzle was falling, and some of the mountains had vanished in thick, featureless cloud. Surprisingly, the visibility into the water was very good, the light being even and without shadow. As usual, Craig began walking slowly up the bank a few metres ahead of us. Whenever he approaches likely water, our guide clasps his hands behind his back to hide inadvertent flashes of pale skin, and slows further. If you're the *guided*, this is akin to a drum roll. Then if he thinks he sees a fish, he freezes like a pointer, often in mid-stride. Seeing Craig do this is almost as exciting as finding a trout yourself.

Often he'll stand still like that for some seconds, neck craning. What you hope for next is the subtle hand gestures from behind that signal to stop, or drop back. This means that Craig is at least ninety per cent sure he's found a fish, rather than merely a fish-shaped rock or trick of current. Trout can't hear voices from beneath the water, so I'm guessing that this soundless communication is a legacy of Craig's hunting background. It's funny how you get sucked into the atmosphere yourself though, returning a signalled thumbs up, or mouthing a question: typically 'How big?'. Once or twice, Craig has opened both hands to this enquiry.

After the first such commando-like exchange on the river, Craig found his voice again, and murmured to Felix the position of a particular trout. I had a peek over the bank too. The fish was one of those rare New Zealand browns that I could see straight away. It was a significantly darker shape than the washed-out grey of the riverbed, swooping from side to side in the eye of a particularly chaotic left-handed run. It was great to see a fish feeding so actively, but there were two major problems.

First, the outside of the bend was a junk heap of driftwood. A huge tree had lodged there during a flood, and every piece of subsequent debris had piled up against it. If hooked, the fish would only have to move a couple of metres left, and the full force of the current would deliver it into this fortress.

Second, the river had split just above this point, and a sizeable portion of the flow re-entered the main stream from the right, immediately below the trout. Felix would have to present from almost on top of the fish, or else this side current would seize his line and create instant drag.

Somehow, Felix managed to creep unnoticed to within a rod length of the trout's tail, and then flick his stonefly nymph up just past the fish. From my vantage point I saw the dark smudge levitate deliberately towards where the nymph must have been, and before I could see the indicator move, Craig had yelled 'Strike!' and the big brown was on.

There is often a moment between the hook-up and the

trout recovering from the shock of what morsel number twenty-nine for the morning has just done, and Felix and Craig had already planned how to use it. Almost as a follow-through from the strike, Felix continued to pull the rod around to the side, and the momentum was enough to swing the fish into the current downstream. Having the trout clear of the driftwood was a victory, but it lasted only a moment. With the full force of the river to help it, the fish recovered the advantage and sped off down the long rapid below. Line streamed from Felix's reel, and in a few seconds he was in danger of being spooled.

But that couldn't be allowed to happen! My friend started running downstream along the boulder-strewn bank with an athleticism that would have done an Olympic hurdler proud. Dodging obstructions, keeping the rod high and reeling like mad, Felix's effort seemed valiant yet hopeless. He soon averted the disaster of losing all his line and backing, but the distance between him and the fish was too great. The line bowed in an ugly arc under the force of the current, and with at least a hundred metres still separating Felix from the fish, contact was too muffled even to be sure that he was still connected to a living thing, and not a rock or stick.

Then, as we all watched, a small tail section of fly line emerged from the water and slowly started moving towards our bank as Felix continued to run and crank furiously. Gradually more grey fly line lifted above the current, eventually replacing the orange backing that until then had traced the struggle.

Felix's pace slowed to a walk, and we could now detect the faint swirls of the trout pulling stubbornly just out from the bank. As Craig approached with the net the fish made a couple of worrying lunges for the main current again. If it had succeeded, I doubt Felix would have had the energy to resume the chase. But the trout had used up all its tricks, and soon it gave up and rested quietly in the shallows. It was a marvellous fish, a male brown of 6 pounds.

The nymph came out of its top jaw easily, and Felix flopped down onto the nearest comfortable-looking log with an exhausted grin on his face. The released fish finned weakly beside a boulder only a metre from where we watched. Craig pondered aloud who would recover first. The trout won comfortably, lazily swimming out into the river several minutes before Felix tiredly raised himself.

The three of us were off up the river again. Soon the braided gravel flats narrowed, and we found ourselves walking along a crumbling bank about shoulder height above the water. The plants that crowded right to the edge were slightly taller than our heads, with significant trees a long way back. The regrowth was new, and only time would tell if it would withstand the next flood, or simply fall back into the current in failure.

Pushing through this scrub with rods was difficult, and though the rain had stopped for now, the dripping leaves and twigs wet us just as thoroughly. Still, Craig enjoyed having a vantage point that gave him an elevated and camouflaged view of the promising strip of slacker water hard against the bank. Light rain started again, and though it blurred the surface a little, it wasn't long before our guide froze once again in mid-stride. 'I think this one might take a dry, Philip,' he whispered, pointing just upstream and about an arm's length out from the edge. 'Drop back into the river, and pass me your rod tip.' I obeyed. I didn't know quite why this particular trout should be a sucker for a dry in the drizzle, but I'd long since stopped second-guessing Craig.

Soon my nymph was replaced by a size 14 Parachute Adams. From where I stood, low in the water and a few metres below the trout, the target was virtually invisible. 'See the triangular rock right on the bank?' said Craig. 'Well he's about a metre straight out from that.' Staring and staring, I eventually noticed the barest glimpse of tail over the top of a pale boulder. That gave me something to focus on. My first cast was hesitant, and landed right on line but about halfway down the fish's back. The swaying tail slid backward a notch, but I don't think the trout saw the fly.

The next presentation was better, with the little Adams alighting about a metre above and slightly to one side. The drift was good yet the fish seemed ignorant of the fly until it passed just left of its head.

There followed something none of us had ever seen before. The big buck dropped slightly back and to the side, then quietly slid out of the water in a single vertical motion. There was no tilt to its body: nose skyward and mouth agape, the brown levitated like a performing dolphin in slow motion, until its pectoral fins were entirely clear of the water. It then lowered itself just as deliberately; in fact so slowly that although I made a conscious effort to delay the strike, its entire head was still clear of the water as I lifted the rod. The tragicomic effect was to virtually topple the fish over onto its back. Any sense of unfair play was immediately dispelled, however, as the trout recovered its balance and raced off downstream, intent on outdoing Felix's fish.

This time, the option of a downriver chase along the bank was prohibited by the thick scrub, while any attempt to move fast down the rubbly bed would surely see me arse-up. I applied as much sidestrain as a 5-pound tippet seemed likely to allow, and bit by bit I urged the trout into the quieter water that lined the bank for some distance below me. The fish spent another five minutes playing 'walk-the-angler'. I would stumble slowly towards it, retrieving line, then just as I got close it would swim doggedly downstream a little further. By the time it was netted, I think the fish had squared with me for the indignity of flipping it on the strike.

We lunched out of the rain in a spacious, comfortable cabin that seemed like a hallucination when it appeared beside the trail. These back-country shelters are a constant surprise in New Zealand: not rough shacks but snug, tidy places that can withstand the worst of wind, wet and cold. The difficulty of carting in the materials and tools required to build them can only be imagined. It was wonderful to sit down out of the elements with a coffee and sandwich at a dry, solid table. Craig lit a smoky fire in the pot-belly stove, and we soon covered the pegs above with an assortment of wet clothing.

For a while after lunch the rain stopped, and at one point it looked as if the sun might break through. The cracks in the cloud and the play of light created astonishing views of the surrounding peaks. Along the relative flatness of the valley floor, and under a smothering mist, it had been possible to forget the general ruggedness of the landscape. Now massive mountains loomed over us, often disembodied. Way up in the sky, the black rock and white snow of a mountain top would emerge for a minute or two, then disappear in swirls of grey.

The promise of clearing weather soon faltered into a renewed burst of rain, this time heavier. I made a mental note to speak to Bob about his forecasting source, but maintaining any sort of annoyance about the rain was difficult because the fishing went from good to better. By now we were on a tributary river, not as large as the first, but still impressive, and more so because the rain was starting to have an impact. The water was rising gradually, though still completely clear. In the fastest rapids, the odd rock could be heard dislodging and rumbling along. This was faintly disturbing, though, by comparison, when a New Zealand river is in full flood, the thunder of rolling boulders can shake the ground.

Perhaps the increasing flow was dislodging food, for the trout were as aggressive and eager as they had been all day.

THE BACKCOUNTRY

I could tell you another half-dozen stories like those of the morning session. Every fish caught on these rivers is a special prize, the epitome of the sight-fishing experience. By late afternoon I was drenched but elated, having landed nine browns for the day, all but two between 5 and 7 pounds in weight.

There wasn't much polaroiding light left when Craig asked me to leave the productive run we were fishing and head up the trail to a special pool he knew. By then Felix had left to rest a nagging backache somewhere more appropriate than waist-deep in a river. It was just Craig and me who headed further up the track for the day's final challenge. Craig had fished this area all his life. Even in the descending gloom of a rainy mountain afternoon, he knew from the curve of the trail and the shape of the trees where to veer off again through the forest to meet the river.

We reached the water at the tail of the biggest pool I'd seen all day – long and very deep. Both sides were walled by mossy cliffs as the stream emerged from a gorge, but on our bank the cliff was just beginning, and it was possible to inch down through the ferns and damp earth to the river's edge. It only took a moment or two for Craig to sight two fish, both of which he estimated at 8 pounds. I could have located these trout myself, as they hovered in the grey–green water well above the flat silt of the pool's bed. But to actually approach for a cast was almost impossible. I had to enter the water to have a chance of presenting the fly, and even hard against the bank the river was nearly chest deep. I tiptoed as far as I dared in the cold water. Then at the worst moment, just as I was settling my last step, one of the fish chased something downstream, passing so close to me I could have prodded it. While I held my breath, it swung back upstream again and resumed its usual lie inshore of the other fish.

I did the only cast I could, a backhand sidecast, and it landed passably just above the trout. But something wasn't right. The fish looked halfheartedly at the fly, then swam a few metres further up. It came parallel to its twin, which in turn moved out towards the middle of the river, and then deeper.

While not exactly spooked, both trout looked edgy, and it is probable that the closer fish sensed me on its downstream pass. There was no point in persevering with them. Now thoroughly wet from the midriff down, I followed Craig back up the bank. We skirted the cliff edge until we arrived at the top of the pool.

Ten vertical metres below us, a rapid poured in towards our bank, leaving a huge eye on the other side. Although evening was close, it was childishly simple to make out the two great shapes that circled aggressively. Craig estimated both at over 10 pounds, and I was in no doubt that I was looking at some of the largest river trout I had ever seen. Then, just as we were gaping at these fish, a third appeared at the very head of the pool, bigger still. This fish was doubly notable for the red sash on its flank: it was a rainbow, and a rarity in this district. We watched as the fish fed aggressively, spurred on by the rising water. Occasionally the rainbow would swoop downstream and snap at the browns, warning them not to get too close.

Each of these fish was in a fly-taking mood, and each was the fish of a lifetime. But the tumbling rapid above was swelling all the time, and was already almost entirely whitewater. Wading into it at all would present the risk of being pinned under a boulder and drowned. The cliffs lining the pool itself were far too dangerous to be descended, and wading up from below would be impossible: the water against the cliffs on both sides was at least 3 metres deep. We didn't discuss any of this because it was obvious. The monsters could not be reached. Silently we watched the giant trout feed, safe from our flies or anyone else's. There was even something perversely comforting in knowing that these superb fish dwelt beyond the reach of anglers. At last we turned to begin the long walk back. 'Ah well,' Craig said, 'some fish aren't meant to be caught.'

(Bob Haswell left the Lodge recently and has taken his talents to a new venture. Something about wine, something about exporting, and perhaps in a year or two, something about a special retreat near Nelson called Clifftops.)

Seven

The Evening Rise

AT 8 PM ON an early December evening, I was standing by the Ovens River several kilometres downstream from Porepunkah. It wasn't quite sunset, as the orange light on the peaks of Mount Porepunkah to the east attested, but the river itself was now entirely in shade. Some fish should have started to rise by now – maybe not many, maybe not regularly, but enough that I could perhaps tackle one to keep me amused until the main event. Better still, I might catch a trout, and therefore be set up with a score on the board even before the short, frantic rise following.

But besides a tiddler that leapt for a solitary bouncing

caddis, the broad pool above my station remained unrippled. Odd glances down to the riffle just below also revealed no splashes.

A nervous look at my watch revealed that another five minutes had slipped by, and I began to have those doubts that haunt the evening fisher. I'd chosen this spot on the strength of many wonderful twilights past. The evening air was mild, still and slightly humid. It smelt of sweating eucalyptus, moss, and the decayed scent of damp silt by the river's edge. I remembered dusks when it felt the same and the river swirled with trout. What if there were something wrong with this pool tonight? Had a cormorant flock worked it just before I arrived, leaving the trout terrified and hiding? Or had anglers unknown fished it hard during the day?

With growing anxiety that I was missing action just a bend or two away, my feet began to shuffle in the sand. Against better judgement, I contemplated breaking the golden rule of the evening rise by moving to another stretch of water at the very time when the action was due to commence.

What's this? Looking at watches and feeling anxious? Surely this is fly-fishing, a gentle and soothing art, free of such unseemly distractions. And surely there is no better time to practise it than among the soft shadows of a summer's evening. Yes to the last, and no to the first. For although fly-fishing is, and should be, about escape from everyday pressures, there is an exception in the delicious stress that envelopes the angler as the evening rise approaches.

Whether on lake or stream, the setting sun often heralds the most action likely to be encountered. Here is a time, not only when many trout-water insects choose to emerge, migrate or lay eggs, but when the trout themselves are more outgoing as the security of their world grows with the gathering darkness.

The seasoned angler knows this. If the time of year and conditions are right, an evening rise is as certain as anything can be in the uncertain world of the fly-fisher. The trick, however, is to be in the best place, for nature does not spread the bounty of twilight action evenly, not even on a single river or lake shore. And of course the second requirement is to actually *capitalise* on what eventuates; to figure out what the trout are doing, and fish well enough that you catch a fair share of them.

And so I stood by the Ovens trying to decide. Companion Ray was upstream out of sight, too far for a shouted exchange of notes. Were things any better where that short, steep rapid plunged into a deep and rocky pool? Different territory from my section: a gently sweeping crescent, blackberry lined on the far bank, sloping gravel on my side. Standing at the tail, I faced west and although the skyline in that direction was partly cut off by Mount Buffalo's bulk, afterglow would light the water well enough to buy me extra minutes before it eventually became too dark to see. Every minute bought after sunset is precious.

Difficult tea-tree scrub blocked easy access to the river

The Evening Rise

both up and downstream for several hundred metres. Only where the almost-forgotten jeep track cut close to the water was it simple to get in. Ray was already guarding the next upstream point, and I didn't much fancy the giant, featureless pool that met the access point downriver.

The only other option was a scrub-bash to the stream somewhere between, and this was an especially uninviting prospect. I had subjected Ray and myself to ordeal by teatree a few hours earlier, having confidently nominated an old redgum as a familiar signpost down to an otherwise impenetrable section of river. About half an hour later, nearly blinded by perspiration and with Ray cursing the risk to his new breathable waders, I had to beat a humble retreat. We left with the river sounding just as far away as it did when we first turned at the redgum.

That memory was only hours old. Unless I gambled on another stooped, rod-snagging shuffle through the thicket, complete with a constant shower of prickly leaves down the back of my neck, I had to stay where I was.

Evening activity can favour different kinds of water depending on the section of river involved, and even time of year. On the crescent pool, my expectations were for the best action to consist of twilight sippers in the flat water, particularly along the bubble line below the run-in, and across the pool tail. Second choice was the riffle below. Action could be expected there, but for some reason the riffle trout in this spot never seemed to reach any size, even though riffles are often my first choice on evening. Besides, the view across the riffle was north, not west, so lack of light was a problem in the broken water.

The rapid-come-run that fed the pool had never competed with the first two spots. It produced a share of duns, and always looked quite promising. But a couple of hard facts counted against it. First, a long-fallen peppermint gum had toppled in such a way as to disrupt all the best drifts with its bleached branches. Aha, you're thinking, just the place for a big one to lurk. Bet he hasn't looked carefully enough, because it's so frustrating to fish among all those logs. Well I have looked, and hard. Maybe the bigger trout do shelter among those branches by day, but on evening the best of them can be found in the open water just down from the branches, sipping right in the bubble line. As for the first few metres between the rapid and the uppermost branch, it had never shown more than the occasional rise.

Eight thirty and still nothing. I walked back and forward, crouched down on my haunches and peered into the riffle, strode back up to the bubble line and squinted. Nothing. Eight thirty-five. Bugger. Two half-hearted blind casts around the tail. Then a splash from upstream. I walked again to the bubble line and stared and listened. Waiting. Waiting. Splash! Not from the bubble line, but upstream, among the logs after all? I raced to the head of the pool, and there they were. Two trout, rising about a rod-length apart just on the edge of the current tongue, and only a forearm's distance from where the first branch lay parallel to the flow. A trickle of medium-sized duns had begun to hatch, about size 14 and grey in the twilight. Neither the hatch nor the response from the trout was frantic; in fact a glance back down to the bubble line showed that the stray duns fluttering along it were untouched.

Why the two fish above the logs? Who knows, but with the light all the more difficult against the creased water, and fading, I presented a Grey Wulff at once. The cast wasn't difficult, but lifting the fly off before it reached the downstream branches, while maximising a fishable drift, was tricky. Second drift the fly stuck agonisingly to a limb as I lifted a fraction too late. My spirits sank. I sensed this rise to be fleeting; there would be no time for a fly change. I pulled and hoped, and blessedly the fly came free. I cast again, just as the upper of the two trout humped on the edge of the current. I could just make out my fly as it landed half a metre above, a faint silhouette against the fading sheen of the river. Then there was an instant of great clarity as a dark nose broke the surface and clipped the Grey Wulff down.

I experienced the split-second reaction of delighted disbelief that always follows a take on a tough day. It's like, 'This is too good to be true; can't be happening'. Could this be nature's way of slowing a reflex strike? Dumbfounding you with the beauty of the moment just long enough that the trout turns down before you lift.

I knew straight away that I was into a fine Ovens rainbow. The river has a mixed reputation both for its fly-fishing and the quality of its trout. I'll admit that it can be a contrary water – as it was proving to be on this December day – but I won't hear a bad word about the better rainbows. There's a class or a strain of rainbow in the stream that is as fine as any to be found on the freestone rivers in the north-east Victorian mountains.

The combination of speed and power in the initial lunge marked this fish as one of them. I was fishing 4-pound Maxima, the trout was definitely less than 2 pounds, yet it was only by a whisker that I turned it before the maze of line-snapping branches. Next moment it sprung from the water, and again the old peppermint threatened to become a refuge for the fish. But the worst passed, and soon the rainbow was confined to half-submerged circle work as I strained to bring it in quickly enough to have a crack at the other fish (it was still rising, despite the commotion).

I caught the rainbow – a maiden of about 1½ old-fashioned pounds, and a fine fish for the Ovens. I could have hoped for more trout that evening, but not a better one. I raced to slip the fly out of its lip and re-cast. The other trout rose again, the disturbance just the merest smudge now in the virtual darkness. I couldn't see my fly . . . there was a rise . . . lift! . . . nothing. It wasn't to me. I cast out straight away, but the trout did not show again.

I wound in to leave, and actually took a few steps up the gravel before I heard a distinct 'clip' come from the blackened water below the tree. I hesitated. Was a single sound worth the trouble of walking back down, stripping off line, and casting out? Oh well, why not? I plucked the fly from its runner and stepped carefully downstream. There, another rise, just the faintest shimmer coming from the previously lifeless bubble line. I cast as best I could in the dark to where the bubbles emerged from beneath the branches (or at least, to where I imagined they did, going on memory). I could not see the fly, but I strained my eyes and ears, and about an arm-span down from where the fly should have alighted, I heard another rise, saw the faintest crease on the water. I lifted in hope, and immediately felt that wonderful resistance, heavy and living.

It was a brown, and my best trout for the day. The torch-light revealed its weight at 2 pounds in the net. A much longer fish than the rainbow, but in the way of larger Ovens River browns, not matching it in condition. Still, it was a handsome trout, and it changed the whole complexion of the evening. Though a brace is not a bragging score for a likely evening on a mountain river, in size these two were well above typical for the Ovens.

I waited a couple more minutes in the darkness, listening and looking. But if any other trout were rising, I could not detect them. I headed back up the path to join my companion, sitting beside his pool, located by the glow of his cigarette. 'How did you go, Phil?' he enquired as he heard my steps. 'Not bad Raymond. A quiet evening, but I ended up with two nice ones. How about you?' 'Quiet here as well,' said my friend. 'They didn't move 'til right on dark. Got a nice rainbow, and missed two others on the strike . . . and just got another one on the black muddler.' This he added with a slight flourish, justifiably pleased to have landed a couple when few fish were active.

Back at the caravan we dissected the evening. Why was it that so little had happened? Raymond had even 'broken the rule' at 8.30 and dashed to the pool above for a rushed investigation, only to find that body of water dormant as well. We agreed it was probably the whole river that had failed to perform, not just our bits of it, and there was some comfort in this. 'Still,' said Ray as he sipped his coffee, 'we got a few nice ones, so that's not so bad.'

Streams are not the only source of action at sunset. Lakes can also provide some marvellous sport. I can remember countless evenings when just as the last of daylight was dying on the water, great backs and fins began to slice the surface, feeding on beetles, caddis or midges. Or perhaps even the beginning of a mudeye binge that might last for hours. Twilight on a lake has yielded some of the largest trout I have ever caught.

Yet when I consider the most memorable sunsets, I realise that the best evening rises of all are likely to occur on tailwaters: those rivers whose flow is regulated by an upstream dam. Despite their infuriating unpredictability, it is impossible to consider an evening on the likes of the Goulburn, Mitta Mitta, Swampy Plain, Tumut or upper Murray rivers without a shiver of anticipation.

These regulated rivers are not without their problems for the trout fishery, or the quality of the fishing itself, but they do offer some major benefits. They often provide a large flow of cold water during the hotter months, which is ideal for trout growth and welfare. And the same flow patterns, coupled with the injection of nutrients from upstream stillwaters, has favoured some insect species – particularly mayfly and caddis.

So you could assume that a combination of thriving insect populations and plenty of trout, including some good-sized ones, would be a recipe for exceptional evening fishing. And you would be right – but only if river levels are suitable.

In the case of natural streams, keeping track of past weather information and carefully analysing weather forecasts allows a fly-fisher to plan a trip with great accuracy. At a range of less than a week, a reliable – if not foolproof – prediction may be made about expected water temperatures and flows.

However on a tailwater, everything can be changed by someone pushing a button on a control panel. While the high in summer/ low in winter trend prevails on tailwaters, it's just that – a trend. On a week-to-week basis, or even day-to-day, there can be major fluctuations in the flow of a given river. That change may revert a water from ideal fly-fishing to terrible, or for the optimists, vice versa.

There is no way of predicting this with any certainty. I can think of a couple of times when my gamble hasn't turned out how I hoped. There was the time when I staked a bet on backwater fishing the Goulburn River in the second week of January on the basis that high irrigation demand would mean high flows. An odds-on favourite, but two days before the trip, the irrigation district was hit by an unseasonable band of thunderstorms dropping 3 inches of rain. The discharge from the lake was immediately reduced so as not to 'waste' water that couldn't be sold to the irrigators, and the backwaters quickly receded.

Conversely, with the irrigation season coming to an end one April, a gentle autumnal flow in the Mitta Mitta River seemed a sure thing. Some friends and I arrived on a Friday afternoon to find the river at perfect height for the Kosciuszko dun hatches: a steady flow, but crossable at the broadest riffles. Then a power station broke down somewhere in the state on Friday night, causing a critical electricity shortage, and the hydro-electric turbines at upstream Dartmouth Dam were thrown into action. It seemed like a bad dream when I wandered down to the river on Saturday morning only to find a rising torrent.

But like an addicted gambler, when you do actually get it right on a tailwater, the results can be so good that you forget the bad days. For a while, the such-and-such river is the best in the world. You can't go wrong.

When Peter Julian and I arrived on the upper Murray near Towong, it appeared that the dice had fallen our way. The December sky was grey and the air in the early afternoon was close and sticky, but the river at the bridge looked perfect. A strong flow coursed down its bed – perhaps just fordable at the broad riffle upstream to a fearless wader. Yet the pools were distinct and smooth-surfaced. This is the combination I usually hope to find on a tailwater – the river low enough not to form one swirling, uniform mass, but high enough to create some turbulence in the steep sections, and to keep a steady current moving in the flat water.

The oppressive weather was a less predictable factor. Air temperature would have little impact on such a strong flow sourced from the icy lakes upstream, and indeed the submerged thermometer showed an ideal 17 degrees. Yet the impact of the cloud and dank humidity could help or hinder. Sometimes such weather creates good falls of ants, termites or beetles (and spinner activity) to keep the trout rising through the day. It may also activate a sporadic mayfly dun hatch lasting many hours. That might sound promising, and it is if there are enough duns to bring the trout up. But equally, the hatch can be too sparse to generate a daytime rise, while apparently 'wasting' insects which would usually emerge on evening. In that case you lose on both counts: no worthwhile surface activity during daylight hours, and not enough emergence-ready duns left for a rise around sunset either.

'Well, I'll settle for any weather if I can have the river looking like this,' said Peter as he threaded the rod, and I agreed with his priorities. The Murray at this flow – about 3000 megalitres per day – was easy to feel optimistic about.

After an hour with various dry flies, it appeared that the trout were disinterested in the surface. This was a mild disappointment, but not one to slow Peter down for long. Work overseas had kept him away from the mountain rivers for a season, and he had some catching up to do. Peter soon replaced his line with a sink tip, and began working a large nymph across and down.

I doggedly persisted with dries, but I was soon interrupted by a yell of delight from downstream. I turned to see a good fish airborne about halfway across the river, dragging Peter's line behind it. I signalled a thumbs up, and then focused with renewed purpose where a current seam emerged from beneath a jutting willow. The willow concealed an upstream rapid – almost impossible to fish itself, but a rich provider of food to the river just below. Three times the Geehi Beetle travelled sweetly along the seam, managing the exact drift I wanted. Memories of past successes on that very bend encouraged another pair of casts, but then came another whoop from out of sight downriver.

That was enough. I wound in and cut across the bend to find Peter. I arrived just as he was edging a weary brown into the shallows. It was a great fish, probably a couple of pounds, and in the tubby condition typical of a tailwater trout during a kind season. 'About the same size as the rainbow I got a few minutes earlier,' enthused Peter as he worked the nymph free. He was trying not to sound smug, but I could tell he was struggling. 'Right,' I said. 'Let's have a look at this nymph.'

For another couple of hours we enjoyed good fishing with nymphs and other wets fished down and across. I'll admit that this isn't my favourite form of river fishing, but after a while you begin to notice the subtleties of it. When you're daydreaming and miss a take, it can prove almost impossible to repeat the same drift. The right cast – one that piles just so in the right place, the right mends, the correct measure of draw-then-release with the line hand . . . Sometimes you can be fishing a particular riffle or drop-off to absolutely no effect. Then you put together a particular combination that makes the invisible fly travel a certain way at a certain depth, and suddenly BANG! There are the fish. Not just one, but two or three from one little patch of river. You don't dare so much as brush a mosquito from your cheek or shift the balance from a stiffening knee, lest you lose whatever it is you have found.

By late afternoon even the nymph fishing had slowed, and with still no sign of rising fish, the decision to return to the car for a drink was a mutual one. I had been standing knee-to-thigh deep in the river for a couple of hours wearing just shorts and wading boots. My legs had a slightly disconnected chill about them as we crossed the paddock to where the car was shaded by a huge river redgum. The cold was a nice foil to the continuing heat, and I blessed the morning's decision not to don waders.

A herd of steers stopped grazing to follow us in the way of bored, well-fed cattle. Occasionally one would feign a bucking charge as if in dim, inherited memory of the days when humans were hunters, not herders. All you have to do is turn and look at the animal and it will stop, a fact you may choose to keep to yourself if in the company of someone you want to impress.

Inside Peter's battered blue cooler, a few pieces of fading ice bobbed in the meltwater, and a bottle of home-made ginger beer was still cold enough to draw an appreciative sigh. In years when Peter manages to get the fermentation process right (instead of simply exploding a lot of recycled bottles) the ginger beer is a little highlight of our summer trips away.

The time from late afternoon until just before sunset is often a mediocre one for fishing in this district. There was no rush as we sat on the tailgate replacing fluids and reviewing the day's events, and – more importantly – wondering what the evening had in store. Some threat of rain hung in the overcast sky, a definite downer for evenings. We hoped it would stay away.

Eventually the sun found a small gap in the grey in time to cast triple-length shadows. We finished a sandwich and another drink, and headed back down to the river.

Peter and I would settle for any kind of evening rise, so long as there *was* an evening rise. By this I mean a lot of fish coming to the surface, and for at least a quarter hour. It could be generated by ants or beetles, it could be driven by emerging or egg-laying caddis. What we really hoped for, however, was a dun hatch (or more correctly 'emergence') followed by a spinner fall. In other words, a rise generated by mayfly, and up on the Murray in December that would probably be insects from the *Coloburiscoides* genus – the Kosciuszko dun.

I've had a long time to think about it, and I have decided that the Kosciuszko dun is the most exciting of the

THE EVENING RISE

Australian trout stream insects. Here is a large, helpless, obvious mayfly that trout of all sizes adore. On some evenings you find yourself squinting worriedly at the surface, trying to see what on earth it is that has all those trout munching off the top. No such problem with Kosciuszko duns. At nearly an inch long and at least that tall, you can't miss them. Even right on dark, there is no mistaking the silhouette of that big pair of wings, splayed just slightly as the dun drifts along the current line. Like stricken seaplanes in an overdone action movie, they periodically splutter into the air then land on the water again. Finally they get the lift they need for a genuine take-off, and fly unconvincingly to the bankside trees.

It always surprises me how quickly a hatch of Kossies can appear from nowhere. So it was on the Murray that evening with Peter. We wandered up and down an undisturbed river for some time, finding not a sign of duns or rises. I've come to learn that *pre*-rise activity is no indicator of how good or bad the actual evening rise will be, but I'm always unnerved by seemingly lifeless water just minutes before the action is due to start. Though the sun itself could not be seen behind the cloud, a sharp drop in light intensity suggested that it had finally dipped behind the ridge line. No more pacing; it was time to settle and wait.

I chose the lower end of the S-bend where I had fished the dry so emphatically earlier, the place where a hidden upstream rapid discharged via a fast chute into a pool that curved from left to right. I stood on the inside bend. The afternoon's failure had not dampened my enthusiasm for this position. It was the rapid above that I liked, steep and narrow with its rubble constantly swept clean. Like I said earlier, the rapid itself was unfishable except at low flows; a cauldron more than a metre deep, walled in by willow thickets on both sides. That didn't matter. The clean rubble and strong current made for a *Coloburiscoides* factory, the nymphs growing fat on the endless detritus that swirled to them through gaps in the stones. When conditions were right, these nymphs emerged in their thousands. Some of the resultant duns would fly off almost instantly, but many would be delivered to the pool below where the trout (and I) waited.

Peter chose to guard the tail of the same long pool. In favour of this position was a break in the willows along the far bank, allowing light from the western sky to illuminate the pool. The water was also the flattest and smoothest to be found for a few hundred metres. Both these features would ensure that Peter retained good visibility well after it was lost to me. If the Kossie spinners showed up at the last moment (as they have a habit of doing), Peter's position at the tail was a good one both for spinner activity *and* for actually being able to see the action.

On the other hand, the number of duns at the tail would probably be inferior. Some stragglers and stillborns would drift all the way down there from the rapid, and some fresh nymphs would ascend to emerge where the tail accelerated over clean rubble into the run below. But whichever way you looked at it, Peter was clearly trading dun quantity for good visibility, and activity that lasted later.

I heard the first splashing rise before I saw the first dun, the eager sharpness of the sound like a wet cymbal. Trout in fast water take the Kosciuszko duns with a messy smash-and-grab rise, as if they hope to drown the dun even if they miss it the first time. Moments after that initial splash, a fluttering dun drifted into sight, then another. Against the dark water, their creamy–grey colour stood out well. I followed the progress of a third dun as it pirouetted along the current seam closest to my bank, and then it was gone in a flash of white water.

I fired a Hendrickson variation out into the seam. It drifted past the position of the rise before it also disappeared in a loud splash. My strike found the edge of a lip, held briefly, and pulled out. No time for disappointment, now there were dozens of duns drifting past, several white pancakes marking new rises. I cast to the seam again, trying to focus on one place, one fish. Splash! Lift! Yep, got 'im. A good fish pulling hard and deep for the middle of the river. I was in a hurry to land it, wanting a couple more chances before the light was lost, but it wouldn't come in. I edged downstream of the trout so it was fighting the current *and* me, and that had an effect. Reluctantly, it moved towards me, and as it swam past I had it with a rushed swipe of the net. Untidy, but effective. The trout was a brown, a young, strong fish of a couple of pounds. A good start.

There were plenty of duns now, and I was vaguely aware

of Peter's shape downstream, leaning into a bent rod. He said something I couldn't hear above the river. Another trout was rising steadily on the other side of the current, and it looked bigger than several closer fish. I was starting to struggle to see the duns in the gloom, and could barely make out the smudge of my fly as it drifted quickly towards the trout on the far side. There was a rise, I lifted, and I was on again. Once more the trout took longer to land than I hoped, and there was the slightest deflation when I beached it to discover it was no bigger than the first.

Just below me, some duns were beginning to accumulate in the slacker water near my bank, and sure enough, two fish started rising for them. The Hendrickson landed ambiguously between the two, and in a few seconds it was clipped off with a rise much tidier than those out in the current. I was delighted to strike into weight yet again – four rises, three fish on. On this occasion it was a rainbow, a bit smaller than the browns at a pound and a half, that was brought to hand in gathering gloom.

By the time I'd sent the rainbow on its way, there was no longer enough light to continue fishing where I was. Trout could still be heard splashing out there somewhere, but now their rises were no more to the eye than a distant flash half-seen, almost indistinguishable from natural swirls in the dark water. I walked down towards Peter.

The glow of western sky reflected on Peter's section of river wasn't much by now, but it was enough to illuminate the broad, swaying back of a huge trout feeding in the centre of the current a few metres up from the tail. I found my friend hunched towards it, casting with paranoid care. I watched two presentations that appeared to be perfect, but apparently the trout ignored them. 'He's been rising like that for ten minutes,' murmured Peter, half to himself. 'But I can't get him to look at anything.' I offered some suggestions. A nymph perhaps? It is unusual for a steadily feeding trout, almost certainly occupied by the Kosciuszko dun emergence, to prove so elusive. This is especially so in the fading light. 'Tried the nymph,' was the short reply. 'Not interested.' I offered a distracted commiseration, and headed further downstream to investigate a backwater I'd noted earlier.

On the very edge of night, a large river like the Murray becomes a mixture of real-time perception, memory and imagination. You listen as much as you look, cocking an ear for the sound of a rise, a sound that is not a swishing willow branch, the slap of a diving platypus, or the roll of a lazy carp. At the same time you crouch and turn, hunting for that extra skerrick of light, the tiny bit of visual advantage that will let you see well enough to distinguish the ring of a feeding trout from a reflected cloud or a pulse of current.

The place I sought was not a backwater in the true sense, merely a slacker patch of river due to the flow deflection of a toppled upstream willow. As I hoped, the surface here was smooth, not confused with current creases and eddies. When I heard the gentle clip of a trout taking an insect, it only took a moment to locate the soft, spreading ring drifting slowly downstream. I waited tensely for another rise, and there it was. Not the rise of a large fish, but perhaps a fat 'pounder' to finish the evening.

I had changed to a large Royal Wulff for its white-winged visibility, and this I cast just above the position of the last rise. The fly did not get to drift more than two handspans before its faint, fuzzy form vanished in another small swirl. I expected to strike into the jerky protest of modest fish. Instead, the rod buckled over with such decisive force that I was barely quick enough to release line and prevent an instant break-off.

The game had changed in seconds, and now I was struggling to stay attached to what was clearly the best fish of the day. My complacent assumption of small rise, small fish had led me to expect a quick, incident-free tussle. Now I tried frantically to remember the layout of the area I was in, all but invisible in the dark. In close, I could make out some sticks and branches that had lodged in the silt bottom away from the main force of the river. I did not want a lively trout anywhere near these, but at the same time it would be all over if the fish made it out into the full force of the current.

Ultimately, the trout ended up hovering somewhere near the edge of the slack water, with me just managing to turn every lunge for the main flow, yet unable to bring it any closer. At last the effort told, and I was able to slowly coax the fish back into the quieter water. There were some nervous moments as the line snatched briefly at some of the many sticks, but eventually I was able to slide a hand under a fantastic brown. I didn't need the torch to see the glimmer of its silvery flank. 'A lake fish' the old-timers would have nodded with certainty, reading the bright, flaking scales as the sure sign of a migrant from Lake Hume. I wasn't so sure, but at over 5 pounds it was one of best endings to an evening rise I'd had for a while.

I walked back up the bank, towards the tail where I left Peter. The night air had cooled a couple of degrees and the mugginess of earlier was almost gone. I was halfway to Peter's spot when I saw the interior light of the car glowing across the paddock, so I veered away from the river. Apparently my footsteps were heard while I was still some distance away, for a voice called out, as it has done on every fishing trip since we were 10 years old, 'How many did ya catch, ya liar?'

Eight

Eucumbene

LAKE EUCUMBENE IS a long drive from where I live; a drive made more daunting by passing some very good – and more familiar – trout water on the way. After five hours on the road, it takes some discipline not to simply detour up the Mitta Mitta Valley, or pull in for a night or two at Corryong. Asking a Victorian fly-fisher to go straight to Eucumbene is a bit like asking a seafood connoisseur to walk past the yellowfin and oysters to sample the crays. Possible, but not easy.

It is the necessity to drive right past some of my favourite trout streams that keeps me from visiting Eucumbene more often. It really does happen that I catch a glimpse of the Murray River at Bringenbrong Bridge, note the ideal height and small clouds of spinners above the water, and ask myself, Why spend another two hours on the road for a 'maybe'? Right there is as close to a certainty as fly-fishing gets.

Besides the bypass factor, Eucumbene is also a lake of intimidating proportions. After a few decades I'm getting used to big lakes, but on a bad day, I still find myself worrying that the trout are not merely absent from the bay I am fishing, but actually frolicking around in another *arm*, 10 kilometres away. Eucumbene has plenty of arms. In short, this water has the feel of a place where an infrequent visitor could easily fail.

You could say that my attitude to Eucumbene used to be something like indifference. I say 'like' because no fly-fisher could be entirely indifferent to a lake that is so much a part of Australia's fly-fishing folklore. When it came to actually fishing the water, however, my expectations were neutral. I was usually there on my way to or from somewhere else, or as a brief detour on a trip otherwise unrelated to fishing. It was always a pleasure to be fly-fishing of course, and my rational side recognised the esteem in which the lake was held – how many million trout was it again that ran up the inflows each year to spawn? Yet the spark that usually ignites with the anticipation of going fishing never really did when Eucumbene was the destination.

To put it another way, I've been known to mutter a fervent little prayer on travelling to the airport to catch a Tasmanian flight. This usually includes incantations against the taxi getting a flat tire, the plane being delayed, or my rods being sent to Cairns. I don't even bother praying for good fishing, because just getting to Tasmania complete with equipment is more than enough to ask. I never used to mutter anything enroute to Eucumbene.

This easy-going attitude had some advantages. When you're indifferent to a water, you don't do a lot of pre-trip research, and you don't have expectations. In short, it doesn't owe you anything. If you catch a fish, it's a bonus; if you don't, well, fair enough.

Over recent years, however, Eucumbene has indulged me with some successful expeditions. There are still some tough days of course, but I now find myself visiting the lake with high hopes every time. For better or worse, the old nonchalance I once felt has vanished forever.

Part of the blame for these increased expectations can be laid on a trip I enjoyed during March a couple of years back. Friends Ian and Tony did all the organising, and it was great to just sit back and get delivered to a mysterious location somewhere on the lake. One way of avoiding the temptations encountered on a drive up to Eucumbene is to fly. We went straight from Melbourne to Canberra at 30,000 feet, and thus had only the Canberra to Cooma creek crossings to contend with on the way down to the lake – all modest ones, though not so modest as to be of no interest to fly-fishers. There was one small delay when I successfully advocated for a twilight half hour on the little Bredbo River, on the grounds that it would be too dark to fish by the time we made the lake. I knew that this was at best a half-truth, and knowing my penchant for night fishing, I suspect Ian and Tony weren't fooled. But at that start of a fishing trip, with the tyranny of clocks and schedules left behind with the concrete and traffic fumes, strong arguments are rarely needed to coax the rods from their tubes.

An hour after the Bredbo stop (which yielded a small rainbow and a couple of missed strikes), we could have done with some civilisation – at least in terms of the road. By that stage, we were inching down a rutted track, trying to reconcile each ambiguous junction with the directions to the cabin left by our absent host. But at last the landmark pine trees loomed out of the night, and soon the headlights were reflected in the unlit windows of our temporary home.

Is there a more exhilarating feeling than arriving at a new fishing destination? Yes, we had fished the lake before, but not this spot. The night veiled everything to the point that the only clue we were near water was a soft lapping sound not far away.

The cabin itself was explored with enthusiasm: a potbelly stove (which Ian immediately took charge of), complete with ample woodstack; snug bunks without the usual banana sag; and even the rare luxury of a bottled-gas hot-water service. Overall it was not a big building, but it was clean and comfortable, with all the character and fittings that a trio of fly-fishers could want.

Before long, bags were unpacked, the kettle boiled and coffee poured. The glow of gas lights was soon matched by the flicker of Ian's fire, and between sips from steaming mugs, plans were hatched and tactics discussed. We talked about the ample dry grass in the area, which could be smelled as much as seen in the dark – a good sign for grasshoppers. The conversation wandered to the current state of the nearby river fishing options, should we tire of ripping 'em out of one of Australia's premier trout waters. Then the lake itself was considered again, and we speculated on the level, and whether it would be rising (unlikely in early autumn), static, or falling.

'Well,' said Tony, 'why don't we wander down and plant a stick at the water's edge so we have a benchmark to compare tomorrow morning?' This was the opening I had been waiting for. I proposed that, seeing as how we were going to walk down to the lake anyway, why not bring a rod for a cast or two? The response to this suggestion was not one, but three rods being busily assembled by their respective owners.

I think we were all taken aback by the 11 pm chill that greeted us as we walked out into the night. What little breeze there was had flickered to nothing, and the lake was now silent and presumably dead flat. To enhance our night vision we chose to walk without the aid of torches. The even ground and well-spaced trees offered few obstacles, and only wiry tussocks and near-buried granite boulders prevented a carefree stride. The dark was sufficiently thick to make all perceptions seem a little foggy. Though the vague sheen of the lake in general could be identified ahead (this arm was more than 2 kilometres wide) it was difficult to actually make out the exact shoreline, where the land ended and the water began. It was more by the splash of my waders than by sight that I eventually defined the precise point where water replaced the sandy perimeter scar.

Favourite night patterns had been tied on back at the cabin. Ian and I had chosen Craigs Night-times, Tony a Sunset Fly. Our night vision had improved by the minute, but it was obvious no more than an outline of this shore's features would be identified without the aid of a strong torch, which none of us carried. We spread out over a hundred metres or so. I chose what looked to be a point of sorts, and began casting.

I can't remember another occasion in my life when I have fished a spot for the first time *ever* in pitch darkness. As I stripped back my initial cast, I began to feel somewhat giddy. The sudden change from work, airports, plane flights and two hours in a car, to my current situation, was breathtaking. There I was, standing on a granite boulder on the edge of an unknown reach of lake, at midnight, with no sounds but the occasional coughs of my colleagues and the hiss of retrieved lines. It wasn't an unpleasant experience, but it left me feeling slightly detached from my present situation, as if part of me were still back there somewhere in a 737, or even an office.

A loud splash, followed by 'Got him', then 'Ahhh, bugger!' returned me smartly to my present situation. Ian had hooked an enormous fish, almost certainly a brown that had rolled on the line and broken 8-pound tippet before he'd had a chance to counteract. While each of us had held quiet hopes of some sort of action during this night session, such drama within a few minutes of our arrival was extraordinary.

By now my eyes had adjusted to the gloom just enough that I could make out the shift in Tony's silhouette to heron-like. This denotes expectant, rather than merely hopeful, fishing. I suspect my stance changed as well.

Over the next half-hour, we caught a fish each, both rainbows around the 2-pound mark. Though perhaps not enormous fish by lake standards, hard, strong rainbows of around this size account for much of the modern-day popularity of Eucumbene. They're fine trout, these. Don't expect to just reef them in, or you may find yourself gaping at a fly-less tippet.

That first night pretty much set the scene for the trip. Hoppers provided bursts of thrilling daytime fishing, the evenings always produced a rise of sorts, and the hour or so after dark never failed to surrender a couple of nice ones to Muddlers, Sunset Flies, and the ever-reliable Craigs Nighttime. One afternoon there was even an ant fall.

It wasn't exactly easy fishing, but it felt right. You know what I mean – you had to do several things correctly to catch a trout, while at the same time never doubting that they were there to be caught. Almost better than easy fishing really.

Then I awoke on the third morning to a situation that

EUCUMBENE

reminded me just how little I knew about Eucumbene. The sunny skies and alpine-blue water had been replaced by a clammy low cloud cover and drifting drizzle. Hoppers, other terrestrials, and even polaroiding were out, and evening fishing was twelve hours away. Hmmm.

I'd never fished Eucumbene 'blind' by day before – not in the true sense – and didn't know where to start. Ian and Tony faced the same dilemma. In our favour, we knew the places where the trout had recently been plentiful, so we could fish these with some confidence. But what to prospect with in clear water during broad daylight? I was aware that the Eucumbene food chain differed from lakes I was more familiar with – not much in the way of mayfly, few baitfish. On the other hand, stick caddis, yabbies and mudeye were plentiful. The one trout we had kept wasn't much help – all it contained was two locusts and some ambiguous green mush.

I started with a stick caddis, but didn't last. I have increasing confidence fishing these little flies at home, but a small, imitative wet needs a response fairly quickly for me to persist with it where previously untested. I gave up on the stick caddis after about ten minutes. Next (thinking mudeyes) I tried Phil Bailey's Aussie Muddler. There's a fly I like a lot, but rightly or not, the only one I had seemed too big and brash in clear water and daylight. I wasn't getting anywhere.

Fly change number three came around. I looked in the box for inspiration, and my eyes fell upon my favourite prospecting nymph. It's a simple mayfly nymph-ish pattern: the old 'Spry Fly' Murrumbidgee Brown dubbing for body and thorax, with copper-wire ribbing over the body, black wing-case, and a tail of dull red hackle fibres. In case you're wondering why I hadn't tried it first, it's because I couldn't honestly say it looked like anything I'd seen in the lake. I tied it on on the strength of my faith in it elsewhere.

I headed for a shallow, marshy bay that had fished well the previous evening, and (surprisingly for water lacking depth) had also fished well for daytime hopper feeders. I was conscious of the need to work the little nymph slowly for best effect, but equally aware that I would not be able to sustain this kind of blind fishing with any commitment beyond a quarter hour. The conditions were unfamiliar, the fly untested locally, and the water only recently explored.

I made an effort to recall the many grey days on other lakes when the nymph had been greeted by pull after savage pull. Yes, I could fish the fly with expectation, at least at first.

My patience was never really put to the test. Within a few casts, I was startled by a soft but definite tug that I struck too late. Two flicks later I locked up on another subtle draw, and soon a maiden brown in the standard 2-pound range cut the steely water with rainbow-like speed.

And so it turned out that the Murrumbidgee Brown nymph, retrieved ultra-slow in the shallow bays, worked magnificently. The only downside was that the takes were very gentle and for every successful strike, I missed two. Even so, I soon had another two fish, both rainbows this time and again around the 2-pound mark.

But here's the strange part. After catching these fish, I recognised my moral responsibilities and ran to fetch Ian and Tony from the neighbouring bay. 'What should we use?' asked Tony as we jogged back to the hot spot. 'Brown nymph,' I puffed. 'Size 10 – very slow retrieve.' Soon we were all fishing together; same fly, same bay.

Now how often have you raced off to drag your mates back to where the *real* action is, only to find upon your return that the water has suddenly gone as dead as a lunar crater? Mercifully, not this time. I missed one. I got one. I missed another. The trouble was, my friends continued to be denied so much as a single take. I called Ian over. 'Swap with me,' I urged. 'Maybe I'm fishing over some special feature.' I went back to Ian's spot, promptly hooked and landed a fish, and had a boiling bump from another.

The thrill of success was beginning to be tainted by embarrassment. My friends were doing everything right, yet I was braining 'em and they weren't getting a look. In desperation, we carefully compared flies. The only difference was that theirs were a slightly darker brown than the Spry Fly dubbing. Otherwise the flies looked identical – and it's not as if nymphs are complex patterns with hidden tricks and gadgets. Still, wanting to remove all variables, I rummaged through my box until I found two more of my own Murrumbidgee Brown nymphs to share around.

Within minutes, Ian hooked and landed a nice rainbow and missed another, while Tony pricked two. I caught the best fish of my six, then slipped on the last take before the sun finally broke through and the action died away.

The eleventh hour fly change seemed to do the trick, but to this day I can't figure out why. We're talking about a minor change in colour to a fly that didn't appear to imitate anything specific. Yet until the fly change, our results were dramatically different. I can't credit my relative success up to that point to skill. Okay, I was chuffed to find the fish and the technique, but after that the actual process was straightforward. Ian and Tony were more than able to match what I was doing.

So what was going on? Did I just happen to stumble upon the precise colour of some unseen organism, when that precise colour (or shade) was the trigger for the trout to attack? Did that weird factor confidence play such a big part that Ian and Tony could only catch fish when they believed without hesitation that the fly was perfect? Or was I (up until the fly change) incredibly lucky, and my companions plain unlucky? Whatever the answer, I doubt I'll ever be able to think of Eucumbene again without also recalling those strange couple of hours with an innocuous little nymph.

Nine

Season's End

A YEAR OR so after my adventures with Ian and Tony, I headed to Eucumbene again, but under very different circumstances. This time I was in the company of Raymond and Trevor, and as our chattels included a large boat, the journey was by road. The other big difference was the time of year: mid-May.

Trevor had been on to me for some time to join him on a late-autumn trip to the lake, and in his repertoire of persuasion, he had stories of exceptional brown trout, and the photos to prove it. Against this was the advanced state of the season. Though only a couple of months later in the season

Season's End

than my visit with Ian and Tony, I knew that there would be an abyss of difference between conditions and climate. In any year, March is the memory of late summer – still plenty of insect life, mild water temperatures, and long, warm days. Only the hint of frost on the coolest nights warns of what lies ahead.

By May, any suggestion of warmth would be gone. Because the mountains nearby are much higher, it is easy to forget that Eucumbene is almost 1200 metres above sea level – a sub-alpine lake. Come the end of autumn, nightly frost is a formality, and the lake temperature has dropped below 10 degrees. I should say now that I went ahead with this trip well briefed on the pros and cons. Trevor is one of the most reliable sources of fishing information I've met, and while clearly excited at the prospect of repeating his successes of previous years, he was at pains to point out the fickle and often uninspiring nature of the actual fishing. But in the end I concluded that it was late May, there wasn't much competition for my attentions from waters elsewhere . . . what the heck, there was little to lose. Besides, in spite of Trevor's warnings I just knew deep down that we were going to have some fine fishing.

The focus of late season attention at Eucumbene is the northern end of the lake known as the Providence Arm, and even the streams that feed it. Whichever way you cut it, this is fishing based on the annual spawning run of the lake's massive brown trout population. It has been a long time since I gained any satisfaction from fishing for spawners in streams, particularly small streams. The main Eucumbene River that feeds the top of the lake is large enough and rough enough, at least under high flows, to reduce the 'rats in a barrel' situation that troubles me with spawning concentrations on small waters. Even so, if I did venture up the river, it would be just to look, not fish.

When they heard I was going to Eucumbene in May, some friends good-naturedly challenged my aversion to fishing the river, arguing that the trout I targeted in the lake would soon enter flowing water anyway, in weeks if not days. They had a point. There was no hiding from the fact that we would be fishing the Providence Arm because of the concentrations of pre-spawn-run trout we hoped would be there. Even any rainbows we caught were probably following the browns, sensing the possibility of a free feed of eggs.

Our home for the trip was a simple cabin in the caravan park. What it lacked in fancy design, though, was soon forgiven within minutes of turning on the heater – it was a beauty. Humming away lustily, it converted the cabin from frigid box to winter idyll in no time, and I was reminded that cheerful fishing trips are usually as reliant upon the pleasures of the camp as they are on what happens out on the water.

As the trip progressed, the value of our thermostatically heated lodgings only grew in stature, for the weather was terrible. We awoke on the first morning to find the starry, cold sky of our arrival long gone. In its place, waves of rain swept down from the mountains to the north, driven by a chilling wind. After procrastinating over a lengthy breakfast and several cups of tea and coffee, it became obvious that waiting for a break in conditions was futile. I donned all the warm gear I could find and headed out the door. Raymond and Trevor decided to wait back at the cabin until I reported in.

Though numerous cars and lighted windows showed many other anglers were holed up in the caravan park, I slipped my way down the wet, grassy slope to the lake alone. The muddy shoreline was deserted. Rather than considering this ominous, it brought a sense of stoicism. And I couldn't shake the feeling that my willingness to brave the elements would prove worthwhile. These weren't just airy thoughts of the suffering-brings-reward type, either. Local lore considered that heavy rain after a dry spell would draw trout by their thousands into the upper reaches of the lake (where I was about to fish) in preparation for running up the streams.

From a distance the lake had the uninviting hue of bridge steel in winter, yet when I stood at the water's edge and looked in, there was invitation. One of Eucumbene's strengths is the glorious, healthy clarity of the water. Even on the grimmest days, as you stare down into a submerged world of sandflats, giant boulders and weed carpet, it seems certain that trout are lurking there, barely out of sight.

Though rain stung my cheeks, and the glove cuffs were already chilling from the steady trickle that ran down my coat, I could sense those big browns, milling in their hundreds like impatient sharks, just out of view. And so it wasn't with despondency that I fished a favourite Olive Yeti in the waves, but with the vigour of one who knows that success is imminent.

The first strike jolted me like an electric fence, being expected yet overanticipated. The rod curved under a solid hook-up, but instead of the following lunge of a 2-foot brown, the subsequent struggles were mere pulses. It only took a few seconds to learn that it was a yearling rainbow not a trophy brown that I was bringing to the bank. I chuckled to myself, half in acknowledgment of the anticlimax, half for the sheer exhilaration of being out there with the first fish of the trip on the line, even if it was a littlie.

The next hour passed without incident, bringing me to the end of the gently shelving mudflats streaked with weed, and onto a steeper, shale-lined shore. Fishing became more awkward, with loose fly-line always catching on the gritty rocks, and the back-cast restricted by the pitch of the slope. Although there was some appeal in the way the lake bed now fell away into a blue–grey void of sinister depth, the fishy weed and logs from earlier had gone.

My eyes were searching the bank ahead for more feature-filled water when the Yeti was grabbed with a confident pull. This time the force steadily increased, instead of giving in to the rod within a few seconds. A good fish at last, diving invisibly down into those wintry depths. But not a monster, for it could not sustain its runs. Soon I could make out flashes of colour about 2 metres beneath the surface: silver with a tinge of pink, instead of the gold or bronze.

The rainbow was shortly resting on the flat shale, a lovely fish of about 2 pounds. The faint sliminess of its skin and the intensifying red blotch on its gill plate hinted at spawning still some months away. For now it was simply a lake cruiser, the small water beetle lodged near the back of its throat showing as its last meal before my fly. When I twisted the fly free, the trout vanished like a zephyr in the 10-degree water.

I hoped that the rainbow would signal the beginning of some serious action, that it marked the location of some prosperous hidden reef, or maybe even a school of impatient browns. But no. I cast for another half-hour with no hint of further action. The showers that had eased returned with increased vigour, and I headed back across the grassy hillocks to the cabin.

That trout was the last I caught – or any of us caught – for forty-eight hours. Later that same day we headed down to the lake to launch Trevor's boat, intent on a serious late afternoon/evening assault. By then, rumour from the park kiosk and spare comment from passing neighbours had cast a worrying pall over the fishing prospects. Apparently it had been a terrible week.

Yet Ray, Trevor and I were still quietly confident of success. Hadn't I caught two fish already for only a couple of hours of effort? Another vein of optimistic logic we mined was the notion that if the trout hadn't been around for a whole week, then surely this increased the possibility they were about to arrive. They couldn't stay away forever, could they?

As we manoeuvred the boat into the water, I turned to a fly-fisher doing the same just a few metres up the bank. Bearded and bedecked in a suitably weather-ravaged and fly-speckled hat, he looked like the sort of angler who might know a trick or two about Eucumbene. 'How's it been going?' I called cheerfully. 'Bloody terrible,' he moaned. 'I've been here eight days and caught one fish. This time last year I had thirty by now.' He paused to untie the stern rope, then added, as if to seal the argument, 'No-one else's catching any either.' This wasn't quite the inspiration we'd been looking for. 'Probably fishing the wrong spots,' said Trevor under his breath. Raymond and I nodded vigorous agreement. Trevor was definitely the voice of authority in our little group, and had been known to catch fish under these conditions before, even when others were doing poorly.

Soon we were planing across the lake in the late afternoon light. Cloud still streaked off the mountains just to the north, but the sky over the water was clear. Despite the bite of racing air and the occasional flecks of spray, it was exhilarating to watch as the low sun cast a glorious pink and gold aura across the passing hills. The lake had changed since Trevor's last autumn visit, being at least 10 vertical metres lower. Some old hot-spots he had fished were now tussocky flats nearly half a kilometre from the water. Likely features had to be found again, and it was nearly dark by the time we settled on a cluster of small islands far out in the lake. Raymond and I were deposited on an islet each, and then left behind while Trevor used his boat and depth sounder to continue the search for auspicious drop-offs, likely reefs, or maybe – just maybe – the amorphous blobs on the screen that would denote the swim-bladders of trout.

As the last hint of light vaporised from the highest ridges, the wind started to increase in strength, and clouds began to blow in again from the north, racing across the rising moon. Soon spots of rain spat at the few patches of exposed skin on my body, as if to warn of the forecast snow. Raymond and I persevered valiantly, casting Craigs Night-times and Fuzzy Wuzzys into the rising chop, occasionally shouting questions to each other across the water. As the wind rustled louder against our raised parka hoods, conversation grew more and more difficult. About the only thing either of us could ascertain for sure was that the other hadn't caught a fish. *That* bit of news would have been announced in a voice that would carry above the strongest gale.

An hour or more passed, and just as I began to speculate on what would happen if the boat's motor broke down somewhere out there in the dark, and what it would be like to spend a night in near-blizzard conditions on a tiny patch of mud, a light appeared. I heard Trevor's muffled voice shout the obvious question to Raymond, whose clearer reply was, 'Not a bloody cracker.' Soon the spotlight illuminated my own little patch of land, and I stepped into the boat with the others. No-one so much as hinted that we keep fishing, so we headed back to the park. My fondest memory of that night is the veil of warm air that greeted me when I opened the cabin door.

I won't spend much time on the events of the following day; suffice to say that the weather just got worse. The 'highlight' was an hour at Three Mile Dam in horizontal snow, where Trevor caught two browns of about half a pound. Raymond and I didn't see a fish. There was a token investigation of Eucumbene that evening, but nobody was keen enough to put in a decent session.

The next morning we awoke, at last, to a fine day. The wind had died completely overnight, and a heavy white frost covered the grass. Thick-furred kangaroos fossicked nearer to the cabin than usual, seeking out green patches where the early sun had melted away the ice. The sky was the deepest blue, unmarked by a single cloud. For the first time since we arrived, the lake was window-pane calm.

Rather than inspiring a mad rush for the water, the benign conditions seemed to create a leisurely atmosphere. With the sun warm on our backs, we set about creating some order from the wet and muddy assortment of gear that crowded the cabin verandah. Jackets and vests were hung on nearby branches to steam in the sunshine, while clay was scraped from boots and waders. As I cleaned a fly line, Trevor retied a leader, and Raymond returned the blur of flies on his vest patch to their correct boxes. Later in the morning we did venture out for some fishing, but the promising weather did not translate into better sport.

The chances of the trip succeeding – at least on the fish-catching front – were fading. Our last evening lay ahead, and with it our final chance to sample the fabled late season action at Eucumbene; action that was appearing increasingly mythical.

Trevor had one more idea to try. Years ago he had found a little-known bay. As Trevor described it, this bay was like a pirate's cove, with its entrance very difficult to locate from the main body of the lake. He had last visited it when the lake was much higher, and wasn't sure if he could find it under these different conditions. Whether the actual fishing would be any better was something else Trevor couldn't be sure of, but as Raymond and I were quick to reassure him, it couldn't be much worse!

Later that afternoon, we boarded the boat to begin the search for the hidden bay. It took some guesswork, and reliance on half-remembered landmarks, for our trusty pilot to locate the entrance, and our first attempt ended in a dead-end. Eventually we located another channel that wound a narrow course through what must once have been a deep gorge, before the rising lake flooded it. We could have almost touched the precipitous banks of mud and granite with our fly rods. Trevor crawled the boat through a path in the dead trees scarcely wider than his craft was long, and up ahead it seemed that this entrance, too, fizzled out into nothing. But at the last moment the valley turned sharply left, and almost immediately we broke out into a wide, treeless bay.

It was a beautiful place. About the size of a football field, the bay was hemmed on every side by forested hills, which offered complete shelter from any wind direction. Between the treed high-water mark and the present lake shore, a thick cover of grass flourished in the undisturbed silt, on which dozens of kangaroos grazed. The closer ones looked down with mild interest on the strange object that had just entered their world, then hopped a little closer to the forest to resume grazing. We beached the boat and stepped ashore, surprised to find no sign of the usual campfires and footprints. This bay had not been visited for some time.

While Raymond began fishing, Trevor and I chose to reconnoitre the area on foot, wanting to get a good feel for our surroundings before the light faded. Already the bay was entirely in shadow. Upon our return, Ray announced that two large trout had swirled close to shore, and just then a third porpoised 50 metres along the bank. Trevor and I abandoned our explorations and grabbed the rods. My companions chose to focus on the wider parts of the bay, while I headed for the top of a narrow arm where I thought I'd seen a ripple appear from beneath a granite overhang.

The upper arm was only a good cast wide, and although a soft gloom was settling over the landscape, I was sure I could have detected any further movement on the surface as I approached. But there was none. The reflection of a long-dead tree lay steady on the water, with not a single quiver to mar its stark outline. I began to wonder if I had just imagined the first disturbance. Had my angler's eyes, hungry for action, merely conjured up the ripples in the half-light?

With wavering conviction, I cast the Craigs Night-time along the steep shore and under the overhang. It landed with a plop that seemed amplified in the cold, silent air and tight confines of the bay. The fly settled little more than a metre from the bank, but the granite rock seemed to plunge deep beneath the surface, so I let the Craigs flutter downward for a few seconds before I began my retrieve. My hands were hidden in thick wool gloves, but instantly my exposed fingertips winced at the touch of the frigid water that clung to the line as I began a steady figure-eight retrieve. The fly travelled well out from the overhang without event, and I began to glance elsewhere, seeking a good target for my next cast.

The bow wave that loomed up behind my lure gave momentary warning of the jolt of the take, simultaneously matched by a powerful boil. Before I knew it, I was attached to a good fish that was tearing down the arm towards the wider spaces of the bay. Though timber snags were generally few in this area, three skeletal trees stood jaggedly in the water near the mouth of the arm, half blocking it. It was essential to turn the trout before then, so I roused from my stunned state to lay the rod on its side and palm the reel.

The trout was clearly respectable, but not a monster, and it couldn't beat 6 pound tippet. Under pressure from a heavily bowed 7 weight rod, it came grudgingly back up the arm. I seemed to be about to land my first fish for two days when suddenly it went berserk, thrashing across the surface like a mad thing, and then rolling over and over. The hook felt sure to pull out, and I struggled to regain control of the situation among coils of loose line on a steep bank. Eventually the fish settled down, and soon after I could make out the bronze flashes as it finned tiredly near the surface.

At last, I was able to slide the net under a very welcome trout. It was a brown, too, and just over 3 pounds – a solid buck, in dark pre-spawning attire. As I admired it in the torchlight, another fish swirled on the opposite bank. Could this be the start of redemption after a couple of tough days?

The next fish hit after only two more casts, this time a rainbow of similar size. By now Raymond had abandoned his position and accepted my invitation to fish the opposite bank. Soon he was into another brown of about 2 pounds. Meanwhile, Trevor had launched his boat and was using the oars to quietly approach some trout that were bulging in the middle of the bay. It didn't take long for Trevor's cry of 'Yes!' to echo across the water. In fifteen minutes, we had gone from famine to feast, with at least a fish each, and more swirling out there under the cloud-dappled moonlight.

For the next couple of hours, the action continued. It wasn't always red-hot, fading noticeably every time the moon broke clear of its misty veil. But for the first time on the trip, we were fishing *to fish*, instead of just casting and hoping.

Finally, the cloud cover cleared away altogether, and the

bare orb of the moon seemed to quieten the activity. Or was it the incoming frost, first creeping over the exposed aluminium of the boat in a sparkling trail, then moving onto the clumps of grass well up the lake shore? I can't quite remember whether it was the first feel of ice on my runners or the absence of moving fish that caused me to reel in and find a seat on the large log near the boat. Beside the log lay a thermos of coffee and Raymond's hipflask of Irish whisky. I added a liberal dash of the latter to a steaming mug, and sat back to watch the water. Soon Raymond walked up the bank to join me, while the clunk of oars in the rollicks signalled that Trevor, too, was coming in.

Before long it was the three of us sitting on the log in the moonlight. The occasional rustle and thump of kangaroos up near the tree line was the only sound besides our own voices. The periodic slosh and splash of trout out in the bay had ceased altogether. It was surprisingly comfortable on the log, for despite the cold there was not a breath of wind. We were also rugged up in all sorts of thermal clothing, with mugs of coffee to warm chilled fingers. While the hipflask was passed around, the final tally of trout landed was settled at nine, and we reflected that in two hours we had doubled the catch of the previous three days.

The journey back across the lake to our temporary home was a reminder that it was nearly winter, and the air temperature was minus 3 degrees. A breeze had sprung up, and the periodic lash of spray on the exposed skin of my face felt like hail. It had been a fun evening at the secret cove, and honour had been restored by at least a modest capture of fish. But as we made landfall for the last time on that trip, I wondered if I would ever return to Eucumbene in May.

Ten

Jane's Fish

JANE SOMETIMES SAYS that I want her to catch a trout more than she does. This is a remark I'm most likely to hear when the rain starts to come down hard, but I just know if we stay for a few more minutes, she'll catch that huge tailer. Or when she misses the strike as a lovely river rainbow sips down her dry, and it's me who's dancing around on the bank cursing.

It isn't that Jane doesn't like fly-fishing – she does. Some days, I'm guessing she loves it almost as much as me (I said *almost*). What I struggle to understand at times is that for Jane, the whole event is as important – sometimes more

Jane's Fish

important – than the result. When the trout is a really big one, or it's a lonely chance on a tough day, this can be difficult. I need to practise muttering, 'It's not *your* fish, Philip. It's not your fish.'

Despite our differing perspectives on the importance of catching, or not catching, a fish, Jane and I have shared some great times casting flies together over the years. Recently, we found ourselves on a remote stream in the Waitaki catchment, New Zealand, and for once I think we were on the same wavelength when it came to a particular trout.

To access the stream in question, we had to cross extensive farmland, and for this we gained the cheerful permission of the owner. Terse signage along the farm driveway had suggested we might not be allowed through, but any fears were allayed within moments of meeting the farmer. He was young, if well weathered, with a 2-year-old daughter struggling to keep up as he strode out to meet us. His neutral expression soon broke into an easy smile as he recognised the purpose of our visit.

In no time Jane and I were chatting with our new friend, while his little girl marvelled at a heart-shaped rock Jane drew from her vest pocket. As so often happens, I soon found myself trying to balance eagerness to get to the water with the enjoyment of hearing a bit about the property and the surrounds from a most likeable character.

After a few minutes, he beckoned us over to the rise behind the homestead, from where he pointed out the landmark gates and trees that would lead us most directly to the water. The stream could just be identified by flashes of reflected sunlight as it wound through a broad flat between high, tussocky banks and willows. Swampy cut-off meanders marked the old course. The flats were quite lush, and dotted with ewes and lambs whose distant communications floated up on the breeze. Behind this genteel scene, however, a ridge rose with stunning abruptness some 1500 metres above the valley. Though it was almost summer, the summits and avalanche chutes were still speckled with snow. The sheep flocks had not yet been tempted to desert the streamside greenery in favour of the patches of high pasture, clinging tenuously between black cliffs.

The farmer excused himself, saying he hoped to catch up later, and we set off. A rough track took us to within a few hundred metres of the stream, but the final rocks and ruts looked too much for our modest car, and we chose to walk the last section. As we approached, the first good look at the water had us convinced decent trout weren't far away. The stream had that impossible clarity Australian visitors never really get used to. It wasn't a large river: perhaps 6 metres wide at the broadest pools, and no more than 2 metres deep. At a glance it appeared to lack many hiding places for big trout, but as we got closer, undercuts, slots, old logs and boulders were revealed. There was also surprising turbulence where the flow gushed between the pools, and into the heads of the pools themselves.

Jane's Fish

The top of the first such pool was as likely as any spot for a hundred metres in either direction. Here, the current accelerated down from a riffle, constricted into a chute dotted with boulders, then glanced off the steep and rubble-pocked right bank topped with short grass. At exactly this point, the riverbed dropped away steeply into a mysterious haze of shapes and swirls. An 'eye' formed immediately below the lip on the left side. Instead of gently shelving towards the main current, it too was deeply gouged and cryptic.

The temptation was to focus entirely on this very promising water, and all but ignore the lower section of the pool. After a cursory scan of this lower half, Jane and I quietly forded the shallow tail across to the left bank, careful to avoid sending ripples upstream.

The left bank was low to the water, which helped keep our profiles down. Polaroiding was difficult without elevation, however, and I sneaked ahead of Jane to examine the head of the pool. No joy. Turbulence, the forward angle of the sun, and a confused stream bed hindered the sighting of fish. Rather than risk scaring any unseen trout, I crept back to Jane's side.

The decision was made to fish blind. It was the only choice really, but a risky one. Without knowing exactly where trout are holding, there is always a chance of scaring them with the slash of fly line – especially in very clear water on a bright day. The choice of flies was less difficult. Trout in nearby streams had responded well to a tandem rig of Royal Wulff with a dark brown thorax bead nymph 80 centimetres below. While I wondered if the Wulff might be a bit too bold on such crystal, sunlit water, it was essential Jane keep track of both the dry and invisible nymph. White calf tail wings make a great indicator.

I began telling Jane what I thought the best approach might be, but tapered off when I remembered she'd fished water like this often enough – if not in New Zealand. Her first casts landed in the lower bubble line, well down from the obvious hot spot. It was tempting to rush straight for the prime, but Jane knew better: casting just a little further upstream each time reduced the chances of lining unseen fish. It was all somewhat painstaking, yet the drifts were perfect, the Wulff riding plainly and evenly in the company of bubbles and the occasional willow leaf.

Eventually, the flies were landing in the turbulent water just a few metres below the drop-off, where the shadow cast by the high right bank momentarily dulled the passage of the bright wings. The currents here were tricky, and still Jane managed both casts and drifts well, working the seam at the edge of the eye, as well as the main current tongue. I watched the white of the Wulff with growing anticipation, yet the fly continued to drift down undisturbed.

Finally, the very head of the pool had been covered, still without success. Trying all possibilities, Jane presented one further cast a good rod length up into the rapid itself. The Wulff rushed downstream, over the drop-off – and was gone! Before I had time to yell, 'Strike!', the rod was up and bowing under the weight of a good fish. Immediately it dived for the bottom. I strained to see the trout but, absurdly, all that could be made out was the white speck of the fly, charging around about a metre down. The fish itself was invisible.

It took a couple of minutes before the trout gave up on its search for sanctuary on the riverbed, and instead rocketed up through the surface. Instantly, we had a full view of a brown: 4 pounds at least, and the largest trout Jane ever had on her line. The fish charged back up towards the head of the pool, then down again, and finally it simply hung stubbornly in the current just upstream, neither gaining or losing.

Now the struggle became a waiting game. The steady pressure of the rod and the force of the current seemed to be working against the trout. Ever so slowly, Jane was gaining line, one steady turn of the reel at a time. The worst seemed to be over. And then the fortunes reversed. Without warning, the fish charged downstream. Jane had no choice but to let it take line, and in a moment the downstream rapid which had seemed safely distant, looked very dangerous. Then, just a metre from the lip, the big brown seemed to take fright at the exposed shallows and turned back towards us and deeper water.

Yet again Jane drew the trout into the quiet water on her side of the pool, and it stayed there. Lowering the fish into the landing net was almost unnecessary. She was able to cradle her 4-pounder for a photograph, and seconds later it was swimming back to its home among the undercuts. The picture I took is a precious record. Yet I don't need it to see Jane right now, kneeling in a sparkling stream hemmed by mountains, a delighted grin on her face and nearly 2 feet of trout in her hands.

There was nothing I caught that day which compared with Jane's fish. I actually blew a good chance some time later by wading arrogantly through a pool tail I deemed too shallow. Not one but two 5-pounders bow-waved madly up through water scarcely deep enough to cover them. Further upstream I found partial redemption in a tumbling chute similar to where Jane caught her trout. A fat, 3-pound rainbow slashed at the Wulff in the most likely spot, then proceeded to shoot all over the place as fat rainbows do. It was an intensely pretty fish: chrome–silver fading to pink on the back, with only the faintest speckles. I was delighted to catch it, but in all honesty it was not a trout that had required great cunning to fool.

Later, as Jane and I were walking back downstream on our way to the car, I noticed the same pool tail where I had scared the two trout earlier. An hour or so had passed – could it be possible that one had returned? Determined not to be embarrassed twice, I circled wide and actually crossed the stream at a riffle 50 metres below the shallow tail. I virtually crawled over the gravel until I was close enough for a decent view, and watched. It seemed that my efforts were pointless, for the whole tail was clearly visible with a bright afternoon sun on my left shoulder, yet I could see nothing. Scarcely shin deep, and lined with softball gravel, the water offered no hiding place for a large trout.

Jane's Fish

Oh well, I'd had my chance earlier. I stood up to walk back to Jane (who was busily photographing wildflowers) when there was a small rise not 5 metres in front of me. I stared and stared at the spot, but all I could make out were the mottled stones of the stream bed. Must've been a tiddler. Then I noticed a large brown–grey dun fluttering lazily down the pool in short hops. As it entered the shallows of the tail, surely safe from attack, a hand-sized head quietly popped out of the water and engulfed it.

Incredulous, I stared again at what I had been certain was empty water. Another dun stumbled drunkenly into the zone, and I watched it with eyes nearly popping in exertion. Sure enough . . . Clip! . . . It was gone. This time as I fixed my gaze on the spot, I was permitted the merest glimpse of a long, dark shadow, almost instantly merging with the river gravel like a phantom. Never have I been so close to a large trout, fully lit by a strong sun, and not been able to see it.

I dared not cast because I simply could not track the fish, and the rises were moving over an area at least 2 metres square. I knew this was a trout that would shy at the flash of a dragonfly, let alone a slightly errant cast. And so desperately, impatiently, I waited. This was no place for the Wulff and nymph, so while I watched for some revelation with one eye, I changed to a single dry using the other. A Shaving Brush was my choice. I'd never cast this fly in New Zealand before, but it approximated the colour and size of the real duns. And there was another reason. The tail and body of a

Shaving Brush punctures the surface film. With the trout barely covered by water, its surface vision cone would be extremely narrow: perhaps it might detect a slightly off-target drift with peripheral vision *beneath* the surface?

So much for the theory – I still couldn't track the trout well enough to cast to. Eventually, I decided to take a punt. I started false-casting as short and low as I dared, then the moment the trout rose, I fired the Shaving Brush slightly above and to the right. For a moment nothing happened as the fly drifted back, and then to my horror the fish was bow-waving after it – almost catching the V of deer hair just as the drag started snatching it into the fast water below. The big brown turned at the very lip of the pool and nudged back upstream with its dorsal exposed. For a moment I was afraid I had scared the fish, then I realised the fin offered a firm if fleeting target. In a second, the Shaving Brush had alighted a finger's length to the left of where I thought the trout's head was, and a cavernous mouth stuck out and ate it.

It would have been difficult to muff the strike, and I didn't. Predictably the trout responded to the hook by lunging for deeper water. From there it gained the momentum for two great leaps, and twice Jane and I watched two-thirds of a metre of trout suspend in mid-air, then crash back down again. It was all spectacular but in vain: the Shaving Brush was well imbedded in the trout's top jaw and only broken line would free it. Perhaps a little too hastily, I side-strained the big buck into the shallows close to where it was first hooked. It rolled furiously but too

Jane's Fish

late. I got my hand underneath the pale belly, and by turning the fish upside down, I quietened it just long enough to remove the hook.

As we walked back up the track to the car, casting long shadows, we were met by the farmer out checking his lambing ewes. In answer to the obvious question we modestly recounted our afternoon. I half-expected gasps of amazement, but of course this was New Zealand and a few 3- to 5-pound trout were nothing out of the ordinary. 'Sounds like you had a nice few hours then,' said our host, obviously pleased we had enjoyed his stream, though hardly overawed. 'Come back again if you like – I know the car now, so no need to call in.' And yes, we did come back. Of course we did.

Eleven

Midges

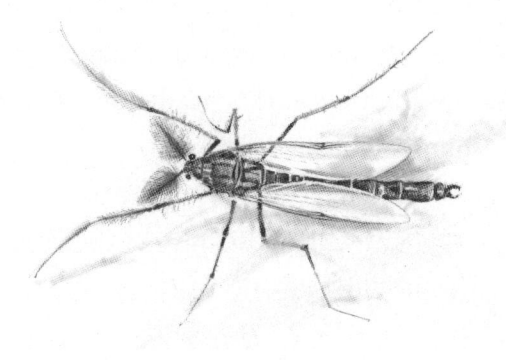

I HADN'T BEEN as honest with Mark Thacker as I should have been. My Sydney-based mate had been looking for an opportunity to come down and visit, to follow up on the short taste of fly-fishing he had enjoyed over summer. But his jam-packed schedule wouldn't let him leave work. As a consequence, an open invitation I had made to Mark in April, when the local fishing really had been very good (Honest, Mark!), was not taken up that month, nor the next. Finally, he found some free days in June. 'Still worth coming down,' I told him. 'We had some bitter storms last week, but since then the fishing's been quite okay.' Which was strictly

MIDGES

true, though I didn't add that it could just as easily crash again if the weather failed.

Then, just before the June trip, a thoroughly disappointed Mark called to say he had to cancel due to yet another unexpected, but unavoidable work commitment. I should have said, 'Oh well, come in spring, it'll be much better then anyway.' Instead, I suggested he come down a week later. This postponement brought the visit into the dreaded month of July – the worst of the year in this district, and hard enough for a seasoned fly-fisher, let alone a beginner. But call it blinding sympathy for Mark's predicament (there's nothing I hate more than a cancelled fishing trip) or call it stupidity: I said, 'Come on down.'

'Will there be any sight fishing?' asked Mark innocently. In his short time with the fly rod, Mark had already fallen for the excitement of casting to trout that could actually be seen. I hedged my answer. 'Well, probably. The trout should get up on the midge if conditions aren't too diabolical.' So my friend and his wife, Carina, came to stay. The first few days were diabolical. Fortunately, the nightly news constantly informed us that Sydney's weather was even worse, thus sparing Jane and me from the usual barbs about Ballarat winters.

Finally, the bitter wind and incessant drizzle abated, and we had our chance. Off to a nearby lake, and sure enough, the fish were midging. I should say here that I had done my best during Mark's summer visit to impress upon him that rising trout weren't necessarily easy pickings. The trouble was that back then, when the rises were to mayfly spinners and beetles, the fish often did take the fly, just like they're supposed to.

As Mark surveyed what I knew to be a very different winter scene, I could see by his smile and the way he rubbed his hands together that he thought he was about to enjoy a repeat performance. 'Right,' said my companion brightly. 'What are we going to catch these fish on?' I couldn't hold out any longer. He was going to find out sooner or later. 'You see,' I began, 'these are *midging* trout, and . . . well, they're not very easy to catch.'

Trout feeding on midges, generally various types of the insect *Chironomidae* if you want to get technical, have been referred to as 'one of the last great challenges of fly-fishing'. That's code for 'utter bastards to catch'. The basic problem with chironomids is this: they appear in vast numbers – think grains of sand and stars in the sky – so it makes sense for trout to target them, and often very selectively. However, chironomids are usually very small, so the fish rarely deviate to pursue individual insects. Why bother, when lazy straight-line porpoising provides all they can eat? Trout are primitive, but they're not biologically stupid. If most of your life outside of sex and not being eaten consists of making an energy profit, it's silly to expend kilojoules chasing something when you don't have to. Just cruise along quietly, sucking in those calories.

Midges

It occurred to me the other day that I have been casting to midging trout – knowingly or not – on a regular basis for the past thirty years. In that time I can recall a mere handful of days when I really gave the trout a hard time. A couple of those victories took place in Tasmania, where trout mopping up slicks of hatched or emerging midges in the early morning seem a little less difficult than elsewhere. I'm thinking particularly of the Great Lake, Bradys, St Clair, Dee and Bronte Lagoon.

The best of these incidents took place at the last water. Lindsay Waters had joined me for a week in the central highlands during March. For the first few days the weather was 'mixed', as a tourist information centre clerk would say. Most notably, the wind blew very hard from the north-west. With several visits behind us, we had learned not to be surprised by this. If you think you're unlucky to strike wind in Tasmania, have a close look at the trees lining the road between Bronte Park and the Lyell Highway. Even on dead calm days, they tilt as if buffeted by a 40-knot gale. It still fools me, especially early in the morning when I'm half asleep. I see the trees leaning hard to the south-east and think, Ah, bugger, there goes the dawn patrol, before I remember that they've *grown* that way due to constant exposure to the prevailing north-westerlies.

If you allow the wind to dictate your mood in Tasmania, it won't be a happy one, as I learned very early. You have to view it as a neutral factor at least, and even a positive. When Rob Sloane told me some years ago that many forms of local fly-fishing are favoured by wind, I thought he was just trying to make me feel better. But I can now see that he was right, and there are many waters and circumstances where it's actually *no* wind that can be a real problem.

Nevertheless, when I awoke on the fourth morning to the sound of nothing, I couldn't help being pleased. We had enjoyed some good fishing in the windy weather, including an exhilarating session the day before, polaroiding the waves on the Great Lake. Stick caddis and beetles were being washed off, or washed into, the very edge, and you could see the trout virtually surfing the shoreline. Some were even stranded momentarily when the wash of a big wave receded further than normal.

But however much fun the fishing, wind wears you down. Having to balance in the gusts, to cast with more concentration, and to shout to be heard by your companion, all takes its toll. So the next day, as Lindsay and I rattled down the potholed road in the piccaninny light, dodging pademelons, the un-rippled roadside ponds and the motionless tussocks were noted with approval. Whatever the consequences for later in the day, a windless dawn patrol would be an unequivocal plus.

I was dropped off on the eastern shore well before sunrise, then Lindsay took the car a couple of kilometres further south. It was agreed that he would fish north, I would fish south, and we would meet up around midmorning.

As I walked down through the silent trees toward the glassy lake, the day had the makings of the kind all too rare in the Tasmanian highlands, even in March. Currawong calls echoed through the forest, and a dawn tinged with frost was transforming into a cloudless day. The sky had the first hints of blue; the air so clear that fire-dead trees could be made out near snow patches on Mount Rufus, nearly 30 kilometres to the west.

It wasn't difficult to sight the discreet dimples and fin tips of several tailing trout even before I reached the lake shore. The fish were typically jumpy, but with plenty of targets and a marshy shore to myself, I managed to take three on a little Woolly Worm pattern.

As the first orange sunlight started to illuminate the trees on the other side of the lake, the tailers disappeared from the shallows as expected. I had allowed quite happily for this, expecting a break in the action between the last of the tailing trout, and the sun rising high enough for polaroiding. Nevertheless, I decided to wander out to the nearest headland for a look around, walking well back from the water to avoid disturbing shoreline that I could polaroid later.

And there off the headland were rising fish, dozens of them. A vast slick of dead and emerging midge had been pushed in towards the shore by the gentlest of breezes from the north. I had a deer hair Red Tag tied on, which bears no resemblance to a midge. Yet I had great confidence in the fly, and didn't hesitate to present it to the nearest brown.

Further offshore, the sickle tails of rainbows could be seen racing through the slick, but within casting range it was the slower browns that worked the feast deliberately. The soup of insects suggested that a fish could simply skim the surface with an open mouth, but perhaps the physiology of trout does not allow this type of feeding. No matter the number of insects available, I have never seen trout do anything other than rise-dip-rise-dip-rise . . . And that's what these were doing, clipping down an insect every half metre, with a tip of snout showing each time.

It was marvellous to watch. The paths of the trout were somewhat random, and periodically a certain fish would simply stop in the middle of the slick, no doubt to swim back to some abstract point and start again. But overall, the behaviour of the brownies provided numerous opportunities to pinpoint not only the position of a particular fish, but where its feeding rhythm would see it rise again.

Though the trout would not move an inch to take the Red Tag, time and again I was able to drop it smack on their noses. I even wondered if once or twice I didn't drop the fly right into the open mouth of a fish that was just taking a midge. Now there's one for the ethicists!

So thick were the insects, they not only fouled the fly so that it sank after a few presentations, but they also plastered the fly line, and periodically I had to rinse it in a midge-free backwater when it became too sticky to cast.

I guess in hindsight that the trout, as individuals, were quite difficult to fool, as midging fish are supposed to be. Yet there were so many of them, moving so predictably, so close to me, that there was a rare opportunity to fire out presentation after presentation that was almost perfect. In the end

Midges

I landed four or five trout, all browns, and that's when the polaroiding started.

The same breeze that dissipated the midges brought a nice, even wave action, and with no reflected haze or cloud, the visibility was superb. The very same Red Tag now fooled classic inshore cruisers, and there were plenty of them. The only dark spot in this otherwise stunning day of fishing was likely to be Lindsay's displeasure – the sport had been so fantastic that I had overlooked the time. I had been operating in some forgotten zone that had no clocks. When I finally came out of it and looked at my watch, it was around 2 pm and I was very late for our rendezvous. How little distance I had covered!

Ignoring the hundreds of metres of ideal shoreline ahead, I wound in guiltily and went looking for my friend. But I needn't have worried. There he was, about 500 metres further along the shore, hunched over intently, and flicking fast casts at what was obviously a polaroided fish. By the time I reached him, he was beaching that particular 3-pounder, and he greeted me with a grin that contained no hostility at all. 'Sorry I didn't get any further,' he said, 'but I got stuck on this corner. The fish wouldn't let me leave!'

There is one more tale of midging success I want to mention before we move closer to reality. This time, I was with my brother Mark (not to be confused with my Sydney friend) at Cairn Curran Reservoir in central Victoria. This enigmatic lake crops up in my angling diaries many times as both villain and saviour, and on the occasion in question it looked liked being marked down as the former. The lake was high after good spring rains, the Loddon Arm where we fished was reasonably clear by Cairn Curran standards, and the day was fine with just a gentle northerly blowing.

Yet we caught nothing. Perhaps we saw a fish or two move, or had a solitary tap on the fly, but as we packed to leave on sunset, the overall sense was one of disappointment. I can take a tough day on a water if the conditions are poor, however that wasn't the case here. Unlike some nearby waters, Cairn Curran fishes well in bright, comfortable weather, especially when the water is high and not too murky.

The decision to call it a day was helped by a late increase in the wind, which reduced the offshore mirror to a narrow strip of only a few metres. I like to have at least 50 metres of calm water before the ripple line at twilight. As I waited for Mark to fold down his rod, I absently watched the narrow slice of flat water, noting that the only sign of life on the wretched lake were squillions of tiny midges. They skated back and forth in aimless patterns within the confines of the mirror, too small to be bothered with by any trout, even if some were present.

Mark had just called to me that he was ready to go when I noticed the midges starting to ball up. As if the midges were metal filings drawn together by a series of submerged magnets, the tiny insects began to clump together in mating groups numbering dozens. Before I had time to consider that

Midges

the balls were large enough to constitute a decent meal for a trout, the first one disappeared in a vigorous rise.

Chaos followed as my brother and I raced to reassemble our equipment in the half-light. I was first, and having no suitable midge patterns on me, I opted for an Elk Hair Caddis of all things. By the time I dropped to a trembling knee on the water's edge, at least half-a-dozen trout were casually slurping down the midge balls, none more than a body length from the bank. My very first cast approximately covered the nearest fish, and in an instant the Elk Hair was clipped off the top with casual confidence. I struck into momentary weight before the fly sailed back with the hook almost straightened. Too soon! Incredibly, the same fish kept rising. I bent the hook back into shape and re-cast, and it took the Elk Hair without hesitation. The weakened curve opened up partially once again, but not before I had beached a magnificent brown of just over 4 pounds.

Meanwhile, Mark was pursuing some fish further down the shore with the same pattern (If it's working, who cares why?) and was soon into a beauty himself. It was a twin of my fish in both size and condition.

The drama lasted another ten minutes before an easterly blew in and dispersed the midges. It was a frantic period, and I don't think either of us fished very well. I broke the hook of the fly altogether on the third trout, paying the penalty for not having changed to a fresh one. Mark's caddis kept sinking: it was a tatty specimen that he had taken off the vest patch without bothering to dress in floatant. In spite of all that we landed another beauty each, this pair closer to 5 pounds a piece.

There were several extraordinary elements to that evening, and although many years have past, I often find myself thinking of it. How did the trout happen to be there waiting at the very moment the midges started to ball? We had fished up and down that shore all day, yet even in the last hour leading up to the action, we hadn't so much as scared a fish out of the shallows. Had the trout travelled to the shallows at the last moment in anticipation of the midge activity, then waited quietly for the skating millions to ball into bite-size targets? And why were the trout then so forgiving of our mediocre presentations and, more strangely, our uninspired choice of fly?

For a while I held out hope that our Cairn Curran evening heralded the discovery of an event which reoccurs with some reliability, if not frequency. Yet many seasons have now passed, and while there have certainly been some evenings (and the odd dawn) when the chironomid feeders have provided good sport, nothing has matched *that* evening. It seems now that we simply stumbled upon one of those gifts occasionally presented to persistent anglers as a sort of long service prize. It doesn't mean anything – you can't analyse it and learn from it. Except perhaps to note that no matter how futile the fishing seems, it could all change for the better at any moment.

Thoughts like that are well held by the midge fisher, who must learn to value individual successes as just that: a win on a particular day, but no guarantee of a long-term breakthrough. In midge fishing, a particular fly or technique may seem to have 'solved' the problem of the chironomid feeders for months or even a whole season, only to subsequently fail for no apparent reason.

The late Bill Ricketts helped put it all in perspective for me in an article he wrote just before he passed away. Bill was already an angler of note before I was born, and was well immersed in solving the 'chironomid challenge' at a point when the closest I had come to fish were those suspended from the mobile above my cot!

Bill's piece on chironomids was written at the urging of Rick Keam. Rick saw the value of capturing some of Bill's expertise for posterity before it was too late. The extensive article, which appeared in volume three of the *Australian & New Zealand Flyfishers Annual*, contains many valuable ideas. Yet a recurring theme is having a particular fly or method work with killing effect, only to then have it fail at a later date. Bill Ricketts had as much time as anyone (not to mention the skills) to come to some hard conclusions about chironomids, and it is notable that his final words on the subject were a question, not an answer.

Back at the lake where my Sydneysider friend was eagerly watching the dorsals and tails of the midge feeders, I was trying to get some of these concepts across. However, I think

Mark may have assumed my comments were for his benefit as a novice. As if by making the trout out to be difficult, it would lessen the damage to his confidence if he didn't catch many, or quickly.

We each tied on a chironomid pupa pattern of my design which has brought relative success – the Milly Midge – and headed for a point that jutted closest to the area the fish were working. Within three casts, a fish boiled at Mark's fly, and it no doubt seemed then that my dour words about midge feeders were a little exaggerated. When that boil proved to be the extent of the action for the next two hours, however, I think he began to see my point.

Though it was possible to look out over the lake and see the rings of a rise at almost any moment, the actual value of these disturbances to fishing success was limited. Mostly in midge fishing you need a consistently rising trout to cast to for there to be a fair chance of a take. In typical midwinter fashion, that wasn't happening at all. Many trout were 'oncers', coming up to take a midge convincingly, only never to be seen again. And the few trout that *were* working with some regularity seemed to revel in coming no nearer than a cast and a half.

Finally a trout did nose into the ripple just close enough that I could almost reach it with my longest cast. Miraculously, it kept coming my way, and at what seemed to be the right moment I drew the fly, there was a flat spot in the ripple, and almost instantly I felt a pull on the line. A bouncy rainbow took to the air, and then splashed around near the surface as I brought it in. It was nice to catch a fish, but at less than a pound, this one was clearly inferior to the owners of most of the backs and fins out in the lake. Even Mark, who at that early stage in his fly-fishing career usually ran over to watch any trout being landed, just kept fishing. 'Well done,' he called out pleasantly, in about the same tone as you reserve for someone who's made you a nice cup of coffee.

Spurred on, we gave it another hour. The trout kept moving, but at some point the swirls became fewer, and the consistent feeders appeared to drift even further out. Eventually, Mark reeled in and wandered over. I took that as a cue to finish up as well. I expected a few negative remarks about midging trout, and winter fishing in general. Instead, Mark stretched and said something along the lines of how good it was to be out in the fresh air on a pretty lake. This man definitely has a future as a fly-fisher.

We wandered back to the car and shared a Mars Bar on the tailgate, absently noting that a few fish were still working, though way beyond reach offshore. 'Well,' Mark announced between chews, 'you said these midge feeders weren't easy, and I think you might be right.'

Twelve

Mackenzie Country

I'M NOT TOO fond of cities, but if I had to live in one again, Christchurch would be acceptable. For a start, New Zealand's South Island capital has a remarkably fishy-looking stream, the Avon, flowing through its centre – the kind of stream I would drive three hours to fish back home. The streetscape and parks are generous: there's a sense that room can be found for things other than bitumen and concrete. Substantial hills free of urban cluster can be glimpsed through gaps in the buildings and trees. And if you find a decent vantage point, real mountains emerge on the western horizon, often topped with snow. In most parts of the world, snow-topped mountains offer the promise of trout fishing.

As a visiting angler travels south from the city, the promise is not immediately kept. Initially, the countryside is bowling-green flat, with a suspicious agricultural geometry to it. Arrow-straight drains, quite stagnant, are the dominant watercourse – hardly trout heaven. In summer, the landscape can look parched, an appearance accentuated when the hairdryer nor'wester blows. A short way out of Christchurch a natural river, the Selwyn, is crossed by the highway. But the Selwyn is often dry.

Then some kilometres further on, the mighty Rakaia River is suddenly flickering beneath bridge railings, and any thought of an arid New Zealand vanishes. The riverbed is over a thousand metres wide, and through this gravelly expanse weave several channels of powerful current, clouded with glacier dust carried down from distant, invisible icefields. It's not really a trout stream, the Rakaia, being far more famous for runs of giant quinnat salmon – 20 pounders and more. But the guidebooks say that trout are caught there sometimes – and big ones. It is futile in a car at high speed, yet I always find myself trying to peer beneath the hurrying water, hoping to catch a glimpse of a huge, dark shape in the silty flow.

As the road continues south, the distant mountains to the west edge closer, and the flatness of the countryside begins to ripple in gentle ridges and hillocks. Beyond the town of Geraldine the slopes steepen, and trouty-looking streams become more frequent. There is a softness to the landscape, created by an increase in trees and the snug, sheltering folds of the hills. However, higher and more desolate peaks loom in the background, semi-permanent snow speckling their summits. With every kilometre south and west, they crowd closer, omens of what lies ahead.

At around this point on a fishing journey south, discussions are likely to begin about whether to continue purposefully towards the destination set down for that night (or that week) or to stop for an hour or two at one of the increasingly inviting rivers such as the Opihi or Temuka. Whichever decision is reached, a bit further along, the road climbs to the top of Burkes Pass, and abruptly the Mackenzie Country lies ahead.

The Mackenzie Country is the name given to a loosely defined high country area in the central South Island. Most New Zealand fly-fishers know the name, for the region is laced with trout streams of nearly every character. Quiet and spring-fed like the Grays River or Mary Burn; glacier-blue and scattered with rare giant trout like the Macauley or Jollie; wide and brawling like the Ahuriri and Tekapo, or smaller but hurried like the Twizel and Fork Stream. The lakes vary also, from the improbably aquamarine giants Tekapo and Pukaki, through to tiny oval-sized tarns – many unnamed.

If the waters of the Mackenzie Country are full of contrast, then the landscape is comprised of two almost contradictory parts: vast, virtually treeless plains; and the impossibly steep and jagged peaks of the Southern Alps, snow and ice smothered right through summer. 'Ah yes – rabbits and rocks!' reminisced my friend Simon one night as we talked about the area. But that's not really a fair summation, and I think Simon himself would concede as much. He is a fly-fisher after all, and I forget how many big trout it was he landed during a Tekapo River dun hatch a few autumns ago. No, this is a corner of New Zealand that is beautiful even by the standards of a country awash with visual glory.

Yet Simon has a point. Even as you are dazzled by views that defy expectation, the harshness of the surroundings becomes apparent. The fertile greens that dominate northeast of Burkes Pass are suddenly gone, replaced by pale, wiry tussocks and sedges. Here and there, patches of true pasture try to eke out an existence, but you can tell it's a struggle. Trees are rarer still; so sparse that a watercourse 40 kilometres distant can be easily identified by the dark-green line of willows that follows it. True, poplars, birch and evergreens cluster around a few lonely farmhouses and towns. But like beggars crowding a drum fire in winter, you sense they have been allowed to exist only through artificial intervention.

The Mackenzie Country can show a kinder face though. On a recent November trip with Jane and friends Ian and Sandy, we found ourselves mostly fishing under a vivid blue sky. This was a point of quiet relief to Ian and me. In hindsight, we had taken quite a risk travelling with the girls to such an exposed corner of New Zealand. I don't know how long Jane and Sandy would have put up with fishing in snow and rain, or the wind for which the area is famous. In the event, their endurance was never put to the test.

Instead, the weather allowed a pattern to develop which suited everyone. Ian and I would depart from our house in the township of Twizel at about 7 am, and head to one of the closer streams for a few hours' fishing. Meanwhile, the girls would crawl out from the covers at a more respectable hour, then walk to the local cafe for cake and coffee in the sun. By the time Ian and I returned late morning, Sandy and Jane were ready to venture onto the water themselves, and so lunch would be packed and off we'd go.

The first few days of the trip were spent on small and gentle waters, familiar in scope to what the girls are used to back home. But the time came when they were deemed ready for some bigger rivers.

The larger snow- and glacier-fed rivers of the Mackenzie Country can be truly daunting in both breadth and volume, even for experienced fly-fishers. However, there is some respite in the fact that many of these rivers are braided. Sometimes up to half-a-dozen significant channels snake erratically across a vast rubble and sand bed – a bed that is itself dry except in times of flood. These channels may be no more than short-course offshoots, splitting away to skirt an obstructing boulder or log, then rejoining the main current just a couple of casts downstream. Alternatively, they might travel for hundreds of metres, so contained with their own individual pools, riffles and rapids you soon think of them as streams in their own right, instead of merely anabranches of the main river.

At times, even the concept of 'main river' is lost, as numerous side channels of similar dimensions compete for the title. So while the brief gatherings of these rivers into a single entity can offer an awesome, even intimidating challenge, the anabranches are usually of perfect size for a fisher accustomed to Australian waters.

The other marvellous attribute of the braided rivers is how well they can accommodate a group of four fishing friends. From where we pulled to a late morning stop under a shady willow, it was only a half-kilometre walk downriver across the fields to a point that would provide more than enough water for us all. We climbed down a steep bank onto the nearest gravel bar, and were confronted with a choice of five significant channels weaving across half a kilometre of pebbles, sand and lupins.

Ian and Sandy chose the nearer pair, while Jane and I waded off in the direction of the more distant anabranches. The usual plans for meeting times and points were unnecessary as we would all be moving upstream at roughly the same pace, and never more than a few hundred metres apart.

We had barely reached the third channel when we heard Ian's excited shout rise above the steady hiss and chatter of the river. Action already! But of what kind? We would wait until later to find out, for in front of us lay our own exquisite stretch of water. Clear, yet faintly tinged with the blue from distant glaciers, the anabranch swept upstream in a crescent that gently bowed away from us. A broad and shallow tail, perhaps 15 metres wide, stretched across from where we stood, defining the end of what might have been called a pool – though it was really no more than a flat interlude in the stream's steep descent. This 'pool' shelved evenly towards an eroded far bank, lined precariously with pink and purple lupin flowers. Behind, and towering into a cobalt sky, were the ever-present mountains, incongruously spattered with snow drifts as we looked up from a valley where one wet-waded in comfort.

The pool slowly tapered towards its top end, and as it did so the current speed increased, and the surface rippled further. At some point, the pool ceased and the upstream riffle began, though there was no clear delineation. Even from our low vantage point, no part of the stream bed was invisible, with the deepest water perhaps chest high where the pool narrowed.

There was no question this river held large trout – or at least what a visitor would call large. Three- to six-pounders were the norm, and you might think such water as just described, lit by an overhead sun and lined with gravel no larger than a fist, would soon reveal any fish. But no. Even after a careful scan, no fishy forms took shape from among the stream bed's blurred stones. It was almost a certainty that trout were present, and perhaps a careful look from higher up the bank may have found them. Instead, we decided Jane would search the water with a nymph suspended 80 centimetres beneath a paradun. Except for its tail, the pool was quite swift and rippled, so there was a good chance any fish present would not be frightened by blind casts.

The nymph we chose was a dark-brown mink pattern, with a brass bead thorax partly concealed behind a crow feather wingcase. Earlier trials had suggested trout in nearby streams were cautious about the flash of a fully exposed bead, whereas patterns with the bead partly covered were taken readily. The grizzly hackled paradun was a white-masted version created for the Kosciuszko dun feeders back home; again, it was chosen as a more subtle alternative to the ubiquitous Royal Wulff.

I left Jane to her spot and walked downstream towards the next likely piece of water. This was found where the stream turned sharply in the opposite direction. The full force of the current flowed straight into a small, crumbling cliff, where the hydraulics had gouged out a deep and mysterious hole. The spot was going to be a hard place to fish because after slamming into the bank, the flow dived deep then welled up in a boiling hump slightly further downstream. There was no clear bubble line down which a dry could be drifted, and I was contemplating fishing a nymph alone when Jane's voice carried down from above.

Jane herself was concealed from view by the little cliff, but her arcing rod, held high above her head, was not. I dropped my own gear on the gravel, grabbed the net and raced up to lend assistance. As I got closer, I could see Jane's line transcribing one side of a neat acute triangle between herself, the river and the far bank. An invisible, though clearly substantial trout, was hugging the shallow undercut beneath the lupins and moving slowly upstream.

The struggle that followed was intense if unspectacular. Jane applied all the strain she dared: first to prevent the trout entering the messy riffle upstream, and then to stop it making its way down to the chaotic pool below – the one I was yet to fish. Ever so slowly, the trout was edged closer and closer, and then without further drama it was drawn into the white silt shallows. It was a beautiful, immaculate brown of about 4 pounds, more silver than gold. One of Jane's best ever and duly celebrated with much laughter, hugs and kisses.

I left my partner to continue her good work and headed back to nut out the problem of my own attractive but complex piece of water. Yes, I decided, a nymph on its own with a tungsten bead thorax would do the job. 'Ooooweeee! Got another one!' came Jane's cry from upstream. Only slightly put out, I dropped the nymph box and rod to bound dutifully back upstream. This trout was not as big as the first, and soon a fat 2-pounder was writhing in the net. Offering somewhat more restrained congratulations, I puffed my way yet again down to the corner pool. This time, I was actually allowed a single cast before 'Wow, it's a beauty!' echoed across the valley. I hesitated, rationalising that really, Jane could probably handle a third fish on her own. After all, she was getting plenty of practice! But then an image popped into my head of Jane losing a once-in-a-lifetime trophy while I selfishly kept fishing. I sighed and jogged back over the now familiar terrain to my partner's side.

Well, it *was* a beauty, true enough. A rainbow this time – probably no bigger than the first brown, but seemingly gigantic as it flung itself skyward in several mighty leaps flecked with sparkling spray. It actually threw the nymph at the very moment I slid it into the net, so perhaps my assistance did count for something. It was fantastic to watch Jane beaming as she released her best river rainbow. However I also decided that with the score at three–nil, it was definitely *my* turn.

I guessed the fish in the downstream pool were probably bored by now with the strange, quivering figure that periodically appeared for a moment, waved its arms around once or twice, then ran off. And so I wandered over to another turbulent anabranch that flowed adjacent to, but just out of sight (and out of earshot) of, Jane's prolific stream. My anabranch did turn out to be a splendid piece of water, and over the next hour, I had my chances and did manage to land a couple of fine fish.

All was going very nicely when I glanced behind me and noticed two fly-fishers of unknown origin a few hundred metres away. They had to have fished for a considerable distance, because there was no sign of another vehicle on the river flats for at least 2 kilometres below where we had entered. Soon I was noticed, and they must have realised they were fishing second-hand water, so they strode up towards me. I felt the slightest annoyance at having 'our' stretch of water intruded on, but quickly remembered that things were probably worse for the strangers, who had no doubt walked a very long way, only to find at least two anglers (and if they could see Ian and Sandy, four) fishing ahead of them.

It turned out that these fly-fishers were New Zealanders, and rather than expressing understandable frustration at their predicament, they cheerfully inquired about our success, said how good it was to see Australians enjoying New Zealand trout fishing, then immediately offered options for getting out of *our* way. This seemed hardly fair, and I suggested they take our anabranches while we went over to join Ian and Sandy. Instead, they insisted on leaving us the entire river for the next few kilometres. 'We'll walk up for half an hour before we get in and start fishing,' offered one of them. Before I could protest, the other added, 'Enjoy the rest of your stay in New Zealand!', gave a friendly wave, and they walked off, backtracking a little to avoid any chance of spooking the water. I stood there dumbly, feeling a bit like a player in a New Zealand Tourist Bureau commercial. These South Islanders . . . if they aren't the most hospitable people you'll ever meet, I'd like to know who is.

At that point, it seemed a good time to see how Jane was going. I located her at the base of a run that just screamed 'trout'. I decided to act as observer, so I crept up onto the high opposite bank and peered through the lupins while my partner worked her way up. Visibility was good, with the midafternoon sun at my back and the sky still free of cloud. Yet as Jane's casts drifted by all the obvious hot spots, nothing moved.

Then just as the fly drifted over the deep slot close to my bank, I thought I saw something – just a flicker beneath the ripple, as if the shadow of a bird had passed overhead. I stared at the spot, hoping for confirmation, but no. Nevertheless, I suggested Jane repeat the cast. Again the paradun with its invisible nymph companion came past, and this time a patch of gravel apparently broke free of the bottom and followed the flies for a metre or two, before merging with the stream bed once again. So! There was a trout. What kind or how big I couldn't say, but I was certain it was a trout, rather than a trick of light or a hallucination.

For the next few minutes, Jane continued to cover the spot – even changing flies. Then something went wrong. After a cast that seemed no different from the others, the shadowy form moved out of the slot and slid determinedly upstream, disappearing in the white water near the head of the run. Spooked! Oh well, there was sure to be another just around the next bend.

I stood up and stretched, while Jane began wading across to my bank. Just as I went to walk forward, I glimpsed a flicker of movement in the slot. Had the trout come back? Without waiting for confirmation, I crouched and flicked a lone paradun onto the water. It had swirled down the current for no more than a metre before a faint smudge on the bottom levitated upward, transforming as it did so into a huge brown. There was a moment when the fish drifted back just beneath the fly, perhaps unsure. Then with the very tip of its jaws, it clipped the paradun under with such delicacy, I took a moment to realise it was gone. I raised the rod, then watched as a couple of feet of trout simply shook from side to side, as if it were trying to throw off a biting insect.

For the first couple of minutes things went well for me. The trout simply hung midstream in the way of the very biggest trout, seemingly unwilling to believe that its invincibility was threatened. Next it made two steady runs upstream into the rapids. These efforts left the brown pulling against not only the bend of the rod, but also swift currents, and I began to hope that it might tire sooner rather than later. Such hope was dashed in a moment as the fish suddenly turned and headed downriver.

For a desperate instant I tried to stop it with sidestrain, but the trout was already nearing the top of the downstream rapid. There was no way I could even slow the big fish now the current was working with it, not against it. A few seconds later the trout breached the head of the rapids, and line poured off the reel. I had to follow or be spooled.

I have never chased a trout so far. Twice I had to cross the river to keep the endless stretch of line between me and the distant fish free of bankside obstructions. Every time I got anywhere near the trout, off it merrily charged again. Then finally, it found a back eddy behind a chunk of fallen bank, and stopped. Shaking and breathless I reeled towards it, allowing myself a moment of relief as the fly line re-entered the reel after a separation of several minutes. I glanced back towards Jane, who carried the camera. She was just a speck in the distance, more than half a kilometre away.

Eventually I had regained the line to within a metre or so of the leader, and I could make out the trout finning deep behind the fallen piece of bank. I braced myself for yet another downstream rush. But the fish must have been tiring at last, for it made no attempt to flee when it saw me, merely moving closer to the bottom. I climbed down into the river and levered the fish towards the waiting net, which barely contained its length. The built-in scales pulled to a little over 8 pounds. What a magnificent male brown – and as was turning out to be typical for this stream, quite pale and silvery, with only a trace of yellow and gold. It wasn't a deep fish, but big-shouldered and solid, certainly in its prime. No wonder it had led me on such a arduous chase.

I walked back up the river and rejoined Jane. She didn't seem at all surprised when I announced the weight of trout I'd just caught – she had glimpsed it herself. The day was turning into one when the most extraordinary fishing stories could (and did) come to life. Yet another glorious pool beckoned upstream, and if I were not mistaken, a very nice run beyond that. But for the first time that day, I could gaze at such water without an overwhelming need to throw a fly into it. Lunch was way overdue, and it was some hours since we had last made contact with Ian and Sandy, though we had glimpsed them once or twice in the middle distance. We headed back across the scree and driftwood towards the channel where our friends would be fishing.

Before long, I made out Ian's form in the distance, running back and forth on the river bank with rod arm held high. Either he was being chased by a swarm of bees, or he had a fish on. We arrived just in time to see Ian bring a 2-foot brown to the bank. It was an unusual-looking fish – a pale fawn colour with only a scattering of the faintest spots on its flank. But it was also a beauty, and I'm sure Ian was quietly pleased that we arrived just in time to see him land it.

It turned out that Ian and Sandy had enjoyed fishing just as wonderful as ours, though like us, they had reached the juncture where 'just one more trout' was less important than 'rolls, coffee and chocolate'. And so the four of us walked back through the hard tussocks and soft grass towards the lone, giant willow that marked the car. I remember absently wondering if I would ever see fishing like that again. Rabbits and rocks? How about rainbows and browns: as big and as many as you can dream of.

Thirteen

Local Lore

THE NOVEMBER DAY looked so perfect I had mentally caught a couple of nice trout even before the car drew to a stop. I was visiting the streams of north-east Victoria, forty-eight hours ahead of my friends, with the idea of sorting out the best of the fishing before they arrived. The theory was that I would then choose the most appropriate base for the remainder of the week.

Identifying the best wasn't going to be easy though. Some Novembers, the stream flows are higher than ideal, with the last of the snowmelt still coming down, or spring rainfall patterns persisting. But not this year. The previous two weeks had been dry, and what snow remained in the region was confined to the southern slopes of the highest peaks. Unless it all melted at once, it posed no danger to stream heights. Not only were the water levels perfect, but every river or creek was clear, and water temperatures were ideal, in the 13 to 16 degrees range.

With such an abundance of options, by the second day of the reconnaissance I chose to follow my heart rather than my head. I turned the car off the main highway and headed up a familiar valley toward an old favourite. At the first bridge crossing, the stream looked as idyllic as I had hoped. It flowed clear and strong over the broad gravelly riffle immediately downstream, yet in the subsequent pool it slowed enough to smoothly reflect the willows that lined it. The valley itself looked its spring best. The trees on the forested slopes sported new growth and blossom, while along the cleared flats, cattle grazed on emerald grass that scraped their billowing bellies.

I nearly stopped right there at the bridge, but instead I pushed on another few kilometres until I came to the old recreation reserve. The rusty gate by the roadside was distinguished from the surrounding ones by the lack of a padlock, though it was as difficult to open as always. The chain had to be wriggled off a bent catch on an ant-ridden strainer post, then the gate itself dragged through the dirt until the bottom hinge popped out with a tiresome inevitability.

A battered sign on a solitary post just inside the gate

requested optimistically that 'Campers Pleese Leave $3' in an equally battered steel box fastened beneath it. I tapped the box out of curiosity, but couldn't detect the rattle of coins. In any case, looking down towards the matchstick poplars lining the river, there were no other cars or camps to be seen. Good. I had the stream to myself.

The first stretch of water produced a brace of trout, which I fished up with a Geehi Beetle – both browns of 12 inches or so, about average. It was a good start, and although I thought the river looked ideal right from the first, it was nice to have this confirmed by two confident rises followed by two trout on the bank.

However, the real action began about quarter of an hour on when a large Kosciuszko dun fluttered carelessly down a sparkling riffle. Five minutes later there was another, and this one was lucky to survive a clumsy slash from a small rainbow. Hoping that these duns were the precursors of a real hatch, I changed the Geehi for one of Murray Wilson's Kossie dun patterns.

As it turned out, a full-blown hatch didn't eventuate, but every minute or so a juicy mayfly would drift down the riffle, and this seemed to be enough to capture the trout's attention, for my fly started to attract a take every second or third cast. In the end I took three fish from that piece of water: the little rainbow and two better trout, brown and rainbow twins of a pound each.

The next few hours provided some of the most enjoyable fishing I have experienced on that stream. Wherever I found the right combination of broad riffle and loose rubble, there seemed to be some duns hatching and the trout were waiting, sometimes in incredibly shallow water. And if the riffle flowed directly into a pool, the surviving mayfly would drift across it and be attacked by yet another vanguard.

Some of these trout in the deeper water were real beauties. One such fish eluded me by feeding under a wattle on the far side of the current tongue, where it entered a very dark and unwadeable pool. A drag-free drift over there was impossible, and attempts to entice the trout with presentations into the current tongue itself failed. Eventually I piled a deliberately messy cast under the wattle. The line straightened too quickly, as I had feared, and within a second the fly began to skate. But would you believe it, the 2-pound rainbow leapt half out of the water after the escaping fly, and virtually hooked itself. I've often had fish take skating dun patterns at twilight, but rarely during the day. What a bonus!

It was well into the afternoon when a rumbling tummy finally pulled rank on the fly-fisher in me. I strode back to the car for a very late lunch of some ham and cheese sandwiches that had half-liquefied in the sun, washed down with a coffee from yesterday's thermos. The thermos had done an admirable job under the circumstances, but the temperature of the brew inside had crept below what could honestly be called 'hot'. There was also another flavour in the coffee that hadn't been present yesterday. I settled for half a cup and watered the grass with the rest.

Call of the River

With the food and drink issue temporarily dealt with, attention turned once again to the trout. There was no question of leaving this river on such a great day, merely the issue of where to fish it next. Mentally tossing a coin, I chose upstream, and drove out the forlorn gate of the reserve, intent on heading to the property of a farmer I knew only as Paul.

I drove up the valley with the sun beaming onto my shoulder, and the air through the open window alive with the smells and sounds of a vibrant spring. After the road crossed a couple more bridges, I spotted the stone entrance of Paul's property ahead. I turned down the driveway to the familiar chaos of barking dogs, each trying to outdo the other playing chicken with the moving wheels of the car.

Paul pulled himself out from under one of the many old tractors he always seems to be working on and strode over. At least my height and a couple of kilograms heavier, Paul was not the sort of person you would like to encounter if you ever crossed his land without permission. But ask nicely, as I had first done many years earlier, and there was always a sunburned smile and a greasy handshake to meet you thereafter.

The day had turned out surprisingly warm, so we leaned into the shade of one of his giant, retired machines to catch up on the seven months since I had last visited.

Now you already know that when the water first appears in the distance at the beginning of a fishing trip, I want to fish

– full stop. Any delays like unpacking the car or setting up camp will be tolerated, but only just. In the company of similar-minded souls, such as most of my fishing mates, many's the tent that has been pitched by fading yellow torchlight at 10 o'clock at night. After all, we didn't reach the campsite until 8, and the evening rise beckoned!

However, give me one or two decent sessions on a river, and the urgency subsides. I revert to being a fairly sensible, social person again, and one of the things I enjoy more and more as the years go by is chatting to the many landowners I have befriended on fishing trips. Often these people are farmers, and in the way of those who live on snow-covered mountains and don't ski, most live by beautiful trout rivers and lakes and don't fish. Yet make the mistake of thinking they won't have anything of interest to offer, and you'll miss out on some insights that can't be got elsewhere.

As usual, I started by asking Paul about the conditions of the last few months. It can be fascinating to draw comparisons between the nature of the fishing, and the seasons that have gone before. Apparently it had been a cold, wet winter in the valley, with two snowfalls at the house, and many more on the surrounding hills. The spring had been a good one though, quite mild and just the right amount of rain. The cattle were 'real good', and the cattle prices 'not too bad', which was the closest I'd ever heard Paul come to being ecstatic about his business. It was nice to see this cheerful, decent man enjoying a prosperous season.

We talked about a lot of things, and I was in no hurry

to get down to the river. November days are long, and there were still several hours left for the fishing. Paul talked of many things: the way the course of the river had changed over the years; the era of the really big trout, when visiting anglers (Paul did not usually fish) would always take a couple of 6-pounders a season. He also recalled the day when, as a boy, he'd taken a 15-pound cod himself on a set line from a hole on his uncle's property, just down the road. Hadn't heard of one since though, which we both agreed was sad.

I had noticed evidence of a recent flood when fishing down at the reserve earlier, and Paul confirmed that there had been moderate flooding at the end of winter, when warm rain fell on a heavy cover of snow. I've observed over the years that one legacy of floods is often better fishing the following season. Mayfly activity especially appears to be boosted after high run-off winters and springs: more hatches, and more insects in them. On this maiden trip of spring, the theory was holding up well.

By now the afternoon sun had moved a bit closer to the ridge line, yet I was in no hurry to interrupt Paul as he talked about floods in general, how they had affected him and his farm, and what changes they had brought to the river. But then he came to an event that, through all his fifty-odd years in the area, stood out: the great flood of 1993.

For those who have an affinity with rivers and trout, 4 October 1993 is a day to remember: a fly-fisher's moon landing or Whitlam dismissal. I was on a plane that morning returning from Tasmania, and viewed the massive cloud build-up from the unique perspective of side-on. A storm was in the making that would lead to stream flow records being broken. Yet I recall that moment for the much less spectacular reason of being one of a hundred airborne passengers trying not to vomit as our aircraft jolted in the worst stomach-lurching ways.

On the ground beneath that massive cloud bank, Paul was watching from another angle. He awoke that same day to a sky heavy and leaden – no wind, not that cold, but 'it had a weird feel to it'. Then about midmorning, the cattle started heading from all over the farm to underneath the biggest, oldest oaks and pines. Paul had never seen anything like it. The cattle 'just stood there, didn't feed, didn't jostle, didn't do anything'.

About an hour later, he noticed that the sky had got a bit darker, and that it had taken on 'a funny green tinge'. That and the behaviour of the cattle finally made him uneasy, and he stopped his fencing job and got back in the ute to drive up to the house. On his way, the first drops of rain started to hit the windscreen 'only they weren't like normal drops, they were like little water bombs – didn't splash, they thudded'.

By the time Paul parked the ute it was raining so heavily that he got soaked running the 20 metres from the shed to the porch. And so it rained all afternoon – sheets of rain, suffocating rain. Then above the roar of it on the iron roof rose an even louder sound: the noise of the river raging to a full flood. Usually the stream was totally hidden from house view by a deep ravine, but by 4 in the afternoon muddy waves began to appear at the lip of the little valley, and Paul could see whole trees pirouetting past in the maelstrom like drunken dancers. By dark, the dirty tide had begun to move across the paddock, and for the first time Paul contemplated the impossible: that his house, more than ten vertical metres above and over a hundred metres distant from the river, might be flooded.

The rain eventually eased sometime after midnight, however, and the steep gradient of the valley saved his home from the tearing water. By dawn, he measured 8 inches of rain in the gauge. The valley was devastated. Looking down to the second paddock, Paul could see that a whole new channel had been gouged right through it. Mud, logs and dead animals littered the lip of the ravine near the house. There was no sign at all of his pump shed.

Paul went on to describe how it took three more days for the stream to recede to something like normal level, eventually revealing an unrecognisable landscape. While he assessed the immediate concerns of lost animals, torn fences and ruined pasture, he gave a sad thought to the fact that no aquatic organism could have survived an event that rolled car-sized boulders, and shifted the entire character of the stream. All life in the water would have to recover from nothing. The old swimming hole had become a rapid, and a new pool had formed 80 metres downstream. And yet in that pool, a small miracle amid the desolation: only a few weeks after the flood, Paul watched in amazement as two large trout rose in the twilight.

The north-east floods of '93 affected a huge area. At Eildon Dam, enough water poured over the spillway to hypothetically fill Cairn Curran, one of the largest reservoirs in central Victoria, in a single day. Lake Nillahcootie, a storage ten kilometres long and over a kilometre wide, had its entire volume changed twice in twenty-four hours by the raging inflows of the Broken River.

Yet by December of that same year I was surprised, like Paul, to find the trout alive and well in most of my favourite north-east streams. As fisheries biologist mate Steve Dunn says, 'If trout couldn't tolerate severe floods, they would have become extinct a few million years ago.'

Looking across the fields from the tractor only seven years later, the scars of the '93 flood were almost gone; you could hardly find any if you didn't know what to look for. The breakaway channel through the second paddock had been refilled and replanted, so all you could see was a slight depression in the thick pasture.

It occurred to me then that every river around here has a story, and most have a farmer to tell it. Another good mate, Tom, entrances me most visits with tales of what he has seen in a whole lifetime spent on several upper Murray properties. In contrast to Paul's recollections of floods and cold, I remembered on my last visit Tom telling me of droughts and bushfires. How the seasons can change! He described the

Call of the River

Indi River, reduced to a trickle by a drought, then turned jet black when a thunderstorm deluge flushed bushfire ash into it from the surrounding hills. 'When I saw the slick coming, I raced down to the river to pull the pump out,' Tom recalled. 'But the strangest thing – just as the ash water arrived, the freshwater crays started marching out of the river in their dozens. For as far as I could see, white claws and brown bodies were waddling up the bank.' Without the same option, the poor fish died gasping in the filthy, oxygen-deprived water.

The conversation with Paul changed back to more cheerful things, and then finally I excused myself and headed down the track to the stream. The day seemed all the more glorious after the discussion of floods and dark skies. Where the wheel ruts met the water was a broad, clear run. Tall wattles grew on its banks, and the swordgrass draping the edges was thick and established. The run looked as if it had been there forever, and only from talking to Paul did I know otherwise. A river may flow for millions of years, but its course and character are no more permanent than the trout that hide beneath the ripple.

Nothing stirred in the run itself, but the late afternoon sun slanted through a row of cottonwoods ahead, and striped a perfect pool. It was long and relatively narrow, with the cottonwood bank steep and lined with old logs, probably laid there deliberately to prevent erosion. My bank was more gentle, with the gravel sloping down until it disappeared in the dark water two-thirds of the way across. I watched the bubble line for a while without casting, sure of seeing a rise or two.

After five minutes, the pool remained quiet, so I carefully fished my way up anyway. Murray's Kossie dun pattern was certain to draw a response – or so I thought. Yet by the time I had reached the top, not a trout had I seen. I laid one final cast into the very head of the pool, and the dun bounced down over the very lip of the drop-off . . . and was gone. For an instant it seemed as if the fly had simply sunk in the turbulence, but nevertheless I raised the rod, and there was the weight of a fish.

The trout felt like a large brown, but it pulsed down deep out of sight so I couldn't be sure. The fish seemed intent on escaping into the tangle of cottonwood roots that lined the undercuts. There was no choice but to lean into the invisible force every time the tail kicked hard and down.

Suddenly the efforts ceased, and the trout swung up towards the surface, then down past me, so close that I could have touched it. Momentarily caught off guard, I allowed the line to slacken briefly. Fortunately it tightened again when the fish moved downstream. I could now see what was indeed a fabulous brown, probably near to 3 pounds, and a great fish for this river. For a minute or so it seesawed worryingly near the tail of the pool, luckily unable to muster the strength to disappear over it and into the run below. Finally, the pressure told and I was able to ease the fish gently into the flowless gravel shallows. It was an old trout, passed its prime, but still impressive. I was able to work the fly free from its top lip without touching it, and only a gentle push of the tail was needed to point it back into the pool. Paul could have a smaller fish for his dinner.

FOURTEEN

The Wee Lakes

BACK IN NEW ZEALAND'S south once more, I sat by the cabin window staring at wet snowflakes as they drifted down outside. Ten minutes earlier, a tiny patch of blue sky had valiantly muscled its way through the grey ceiling that stretched like an old tarp from horizon to horizon. This patch of blue had been the motivation I needed to put the coffee cup down and start dressing in the many layers 3 degrees of late afternoon temperature would require. But then the sleet and snow had come drifting in once more from the Ben Ohau Range, quietly covering the gleaming white lower slopes like a shroud. Was it really worth fishing in these conditions, or was I just being stubborn?

My companions seemed well settled into books and fly-box tidying, just chuckling and shaking their heads when I asked for a volunteer to join me. I opened the back door to load the rod into the car, and was met by a particularly icy blast that splashed my face with half-melted snowflakes. Again I hesitated, stuck on the threshold between the warm aura of the cabin and a moderate high plains blizzard. But bugger it, how often did I get to fish this incredible area, even if the weather was uninviting?

I mentally pictured myself in two weeks' time, back in the real world, racing from one wretched chore to another. Perhaps then I would stop for a moment, and my mind would briefly wander. Between the ring of mobile phone and the stupid ping-pong gurgle of email log-on, would I recall my slothful attitude in foregoing a few hours on some of the best water in the world?

One thing about fishing in wet snowstorms – at least you have the water all to yourself. As I drove down the road towards my destination, it was easy to imagine I was the sole survivor of some dreadful plague, so deserted were the surroundings. The foothills of the Ben Ohau Range are not overrun with people at the best of times. On a dreary weekday afternoon, not another car did I see, nor a single wisp of smoke from the few lonely farmhouses I passed.

A scattering of small ponds or tarns lie in the foothills of the Ben Ohau. Some are named, some are not. For others, it depends on who you ask. With numerous blue-ribbon rivers and majestic lakes nearby, these baby stillwaters seem to be of little interest to most anglers. And yet during earlier investigations I'd established that even the most improbable ponds contained trout, and good ones too. Like the trout of Tasmania's Central Plateau, it seems the local fish will migrate up the tiniest runnels in search of new waters to populate.

So many were the wee lakes I had 'discovered', there was a confusion of choice. Over the next half-hour indecision kept me in the car as I trundled back and forth past various waters, trying to pick the right one. Some appeared uninvitingly barren, mere holes full of water encircled by tussocks and stones. Other waters were prettier, featuring irregular shorelines patched with willow thickets and poplars. They certainly offered a modicum of shelter, but would they offer superior fish?

I decided to start on an exposed lake, then retire to a more sheltered one. Parking the car on a hilltop gravel verge, I climbed from the warm cocoon into the full brunt of a particularly nasty sleet storm. Jacket hood pulled tight, I made my way down a snowgrass slope towards the cold grey pond. It was a bitter late afternoon. The cloud, which had all but enveloped the mountains ahead, lifted momentarily. I could see the snow had crept still further down the slopes, and now appeared to be almost at the same level as my present position.

The Wee Lakes

Besides the likelihood of solitude, another point in favour of fishing in bad weather is that it seems to make the fish more fearless, and not a little careless. I use both words in the relative sense – these are trout we're talking about. However, no sooner did I find myself standing on the rocky lakeside wondering what to do next, than a large, dark shape cruised casually past. It was so close I could have poked it with the rod.

On a fine day, I would have scared that fish – and probably never known it. I had approached over elevated, open ground without stealth. Yet with a wind-whipped surface, low light, and no angler visits for days or even weeks, perhaps the trout had switched off the part of its brain devoted to danger – or at least turned it to 'low'.

There was something else encouraging about the trout: it had a busy look. You know the kind of fish. Not cruising aimlessly, but on the job. A little tail flick here, a dart to the bottom there. The visibility wasn't good enough to actually see it eat things, but this was clearly a trout that was hunting. And such fish can be caught.

I had expected to spend some minutes examining the water and looking for inspiration before choosing a fly, but with a big trout moving away into the gloom, there wasn't time. A Royal Wulff graced the tippet, a relic of stream fishing earlier. While a great fly for swift water, I have less faith in this pattern on lakes. Nevertheless, I paced down the shore after the departing fish, and placed the Wulff slightly short, just over its tail. Somehow, in all the chop and ripple, the trout detected the landing fly, turned 180 degrees, and took it savagely. I didn't even get a chance to lift the rod before the fish turned abruptly back to resume its patrol and the line was tight. With its simple plans unexpectedly thwarted, the trout charged out into the lake in a series of enraged leaps.

I was almost broken off right then, having lagged one step behind the action in a sort of hypothermic daze. This was a fine fish: a thick-set male brown of at least 5 pounds. And yet the line held just long enough, before I came out of my stupor and let the fish run. Away it went, trailing line through the foam-streaked wavelets. The structure of this tarn was a mystery; I had no idea if weed or some other obstacle lurked beneath the surface. It was academic anyway – there was no chance of diverting the fish from its course, at least not at first.

If there were weed beds or snags down in those frigid depths, the brown didn't reach them. For all its ferocity and head shaking, it could find no obstruction to help its cause. The strength of its lunges gradually ebbed, and eventually I led the fish onto a little wave-washed beach.

How quickly the demeanour of a trip can change! Minutes earlier I'd been cold and distracted. Now I was *fishing* – alert and fully functional. If anything though, the weather had gotten worse, and another sleety shower buffeted the tarn as I resumed my search for another fish. Horizontal ice forced a backward walk, so that my hood took the brunt of the storm, not my face. It was still an hour until sunset, yet already a grey twilight seemed to envelop the landscape, the cloud now so low that even the small hill above the lake was brushed by swirls of mist.

As the sleet turned to wet snow again, it was tolerable to face into the wind, and up the lake shore. Though the light was poor and my polaroids blotched with water, still the visibility along the lakeshore was surprisingly good. A pale, clay-coloured strip of clean-swept substrate hugged the bank like a submerged track before giving way to a darker and more mysterious lake bed further out. The uniform dullness of the sky ensured there were no white reflections to retard the view into the water. Combined, the unlikely result was that I could polaroid 50 metres or more ahead – or at least I could within the inshore strip.

And almost straight away, there was another shape, a long cast up the bank and moving fast towards me. Once or twice, it swerved out into deeper water and vanished, but mostly it was quite easy to see. I crouched and cast the Wulff up the shore so it lay in wait, bobbing only an arm-span from the bank. Even from low down, I could make out the approaching smudge of the trout, periodically darting to either side for some invisible prey. Then it spotted the fly from two rod lengths, and sped straight toward it. Another take seemed certain, but at the last moment, with its nose almost touching the fly, the fish braked with a swirl of water. Agitated but apparently unsure, it circled the Wulff twice, as if to examine it from all angles. And then it swam on, leaving the fly sitting on the dark wavelets, rejected.

Earlier misgivings about a rushed choice of fly – or

rather, a *non* choice – now began to look justified. Not for the first time, I reflected on the phenomena of the Royal Wulff, a fly that has become part of trout-angling folklore. The beguiling sheen of its peacock herl body, divided by a shimmer of scarlet silk and coupled with a bold white wing, were already features of the successful Royal Coachman. But Lee Wulff's substitution of bucktail for the wings and tail added durability, buoyancy and a general robustness. Today, the Royal Wulff stands in the minds of some as little less than a magician's work, so strongly can it pull the hapless trout. I know several competent and experienced stream anglers who scarcely use another dry fly.

Yet in the Royal Wulff's strength lies also its weakness. If a fish gets to look at the fly too closely and for too long, often something goes wrong. It is almost as if this delicious morsel suddenly appears too good to be true, too fantastic to be safe. I imagine I've seen trout in inner turmoil over Royal Wulffs; their greed fighting with their caution.

And so it was with the large brown cruising the tarn shore. I cast the Wulff again at its departing shape, but this time the trout avoided it with cold indifference, and perhaps even a touch of fear. The spell was well and truly broken. I was forced to do what circumstances had so far postponed: make a considered choice of fly. But what fly? There were no obvious clues. On a sleet-lashed high country afternoon, not so much as a midge ventured forth. And yet this little lake plainly had the food supply to grow big trout, some of which were out hunting even under Arctic conditions.

The Wee Lakes

It was time to go back to the basics of fly-fishing, to actually search along the lake margin for whatever it was that the trout were seeking. Kneeling in the shallows, I began turning over stones with rapidly numbing fingers, and soon I found a possible answer. Damselfly nymphs. Squatter and darker than those around home, the inch-long insects were surprisingly abundant for such an inhospitable environment. I searched my fly boxes, gratified to find I'd brought my damsel nymph patterns with me. None were really dark enough, but a couple were almost the right size, or at least they would be with a little marabou trimmed from the tail.

I contemplated fishing a nymph alone, but thoughts of the first fish persuaded me to fish a damsel in tandem with the Royal Wulff. Soon I was rigged up and ready again. The damsel dangling 2 feet beneath the Wulff offered new confidence.

The second fish was long gone of course, but I kept moving up the bank, hoping and indeed expecting another chance. Another ten minutes and 200 metres passed without further movement along the inshore highway. With some unease, I turned back towards the scene of the earlier action. The subsurface view wasn't as good walking in the direction of the sun, even a sun well-hidden somewhere up above the cloud. However, at least I had the weather at my back.

As I approached the rocky point where I had seen the second fish, I began to walk slower and look harder . . . but too late I saw faint movement just outside the pale 'road', and barely visible through the foggy glare of a low and storm-bound sun. There was no chance to cast. I simply froze, and hoped the fish would fail to notice this sudden addition to the landscape. A forlorn hope it seemed, for as the trout came parallel to me, so close I could see the spots and its peering eye, it veered determinedly offshore. In a blink it was just the faintest departing blur against the deeper, darker water. Yet I cast anyway, throwing the damsel and Wulff across the wind and in the direction of the big brown – and at the same moment, the fish disappeared from sight completely.

Once again, the bright wings bobbed untouched on the black waves. No, it was a futile gesture to cast at a trout that was almost certainly scared. Probably the same one which refused the fly earlier. Then the little white buoy suddenly vanished, and for the second time that day, the line was tight before my slow wits could raise the rod. In an instant, a lovely brown was tail-walking way out in the white caps. The last metres of fly line popped out through the rod tip, and there was a moment to reflect that when these tarn trout *did* decide to take the fly, there was no mucking around.

At length the fish stopped its headlong rush for the far side of the lake, and I began to recover backing onto the reel, followed a little later and with some relief by the fly line.

As if the trout had summoned the elements in its defence, the wind really began to blow. Soon the line between the rod and the fish started to curve like a loaded longbow, despite tension at the very edge of the tippet's strength. With no grove of trees to shelter behind, or steep headland to break the force of its gathering strength, the gale's full force bowed me to my knees. When eventually the trout was rolling in the shallows, the line was making a high-pitched whirring noise, and gusts were tearing sheets of water right off the tarn and flinging them onto the shore. I had a brief moment to admire a fine brown as I worked the damsel nymph free: a fish almost identical to the first save for a deep scar on its left side. But even as I released it, the storm pushed icy spray into previously dry corners beneath jacket and waders. Without a backward glance, I turned away from the water and staggered up the slope to the car. I opened the passenger door, threw rod and dripping jacket over the back seat, then jumped in and slammed the door shut.

I took a few moments to catch my breath, lying back in the seat while the moaning gale rocked the car. I had been in no danger – there was nothing of any substance to blow into or onto me in the sparse landscape. And yet there was a sense of almost delicious relief to be once again snugly inside the steel cocoon. I reached over for my jacket and rummaged through the many pockets. And yes! There was a very promising lump in one. After a couple of false leads, I pulled out a chocolate bar that had probably lain there for two or three days, and peeled back the wrapper. The slightly melted-and-reset look was no deterrent, and I savoured a luxurious bite.

On the walk up the hill, there had been no contemplation of further fishing that day. The wind, which had been merely uncomfortable to work in earlier, was now impossible. The water surface had become so foam-streaked, continued sight fishing was out. Besides, I was beginning to form a very satisfying mental image of my Shackleton-like form bursting through the cabin door in snow-dusted beanie and gloves, grim, but vindicated by the capture of two fine trout. 'Yep,' I would tell my companions in a slightly accusatory tone, 'the sort of fish you don't see in these tarns during *fine* weather.'

Whether it was an endorphin-releasing agent in the chocolate, or the giddy sense of wellbeing that came from being out of the storm, I soon found myself reconsidering one more session with the rod. Not on the tarn just fished, which looked as inhospitable as when I left it. But what about the little lake just down the road, the one with trees on the banks? No harm in looking.

After a kilometre or so, I detoured onto a side track. It was marked by a wooden sign neatly snapped in two, so it announced ambiguously 'LAKE PO . . .'. There was no trace of the missing half, which, judging by the day's weather, had perhaps blown into another part of New Zealand. The track was rough, but it had the great advantage, on a wild day, of travelling all the way to the water's edge.

The mysterious Lake Po . . . was indeed as solidly ringed by trees as it appeared from the main road: primarily short, thick-set willows that had wisely decided to grow out rather than up. The lake was also confined by steep slopes on all but one side, and the overall effect was that the wind speed by the water was significantly reduced. Yes, definitely worth ten minutes.

The Wee Lakes

I re-applied jacket, gloves and beanie, grabbed the rod, and set off for a look. A faintly pink tinge to the woolly clouds suggested that somewhere the sun was setting. Blasts of wind still blew down off the hills with ominous force, but the sleet and snow had ceased for the moment. After a hundred metres, the shoreline turned sharply right, and formed the mouth of a small horse-shoe bay. I walked through a gap in the willows and for the first time that afternoon, found myself facing calm water. It is true that periodic gusts still found their way in, swirling willow leaves across the surface. But in between, the bay was mirror calm. And clear. So clear, that even in post sunset dimness, the creamy-white silt lining the lake bed seemed almost to glow. The silt was patched with small clumps of dark weed, yet even so, I had the omnipotent sensation of knowing that if a trout swam past anywhere in a 50-metre radius, I would see it. I cannot really explain why the visibility was so extraordinary. Perhaps it was partly due to the whiteness of the silt, and the dark reflections of the willows on the opposite bank. Whatever, by comparison, the previous tarn was a murky mystery. Never, not even on the clearest lakes on the sunniest, bluest days, have I experienced such certainty: if there were a trout in this bay, I would know it soon enough.

And you can guess already, there was. A 4-pounder, and a rainbow this time, busy as could be. Darting with complete confidence into the weed patches, out over the silt, swerving back into the weed again. I almost felt guilty, like a voyeur behind one-way glass. So obviously confident was the rainbow of its invisibility in the twilight – and so mistaken.

For all its zigging and zagging, the fish was transcribing a rough arc across the bay, and it wasn't difficult to anticipate its next position. I placed the Wulff and damsel team about 10 metres ahead of the rainbow, and waited. It spotted the flies from 5 metres away, and raced at them with single-minded purpose. I honestly think it took both, for I'm sure it gulped the Wulff, yet it turned out to be firmly hooked on the damsel alone. At once it tore off across the flats, visible as a bold dark shape the whole time, though it never jumped. It dived instead, ploughing through any weed clumps it could find. Fortunately, these were quite fragile, and parted around the line. There was one anxious moment when the fish was headed for an old willow skeleton at the head of the bay, but it turned back again of its own accord.

The steep lip of the bank offered no place to beach the rainbow, so I drew the net out. Perhaps impatiently, I swept the fish up on the first pass. What a lovely trout – silvery with only the faintest tinge of crimson – probably a maiden fish. I was vaguely surprised at how light its coloration was, given the fish's dark appearance in the water.

With the hook removed, the rainbow glided quietly from the net. I traced its path as it swam out across the bay, then into the lake proper. It must have been nearly 80 metres away before it finally melted into the gloom. So, there was still enough light to perhaps find another, and of course I thought

The Wee Lakes

about it. But even as I stood there, the damp spots beneath the jacket and around my sleeves chilled again in a gust of wind. I had some stories for my companions, tucked snugly indoors – more than I could have hoped for. I pulled myself away from the wee lake, and as the first star winked through a hole in the cloud, I arrived back at the cabin.

Fifteen

The Creek

There is a certain creek flowing through the central highlands of Victoria, and this creek and I go back a long way. By most standards, it is nothing special. Just another stream that has lived a little too close to European man for a little too long. Many sections are infested with blackberry, willow and furze bush. In between, the banks are eroded, which in turn silts up some of the pools. In summer, too much of the creek's water ends up in washing machines and on gardens. For all that, the trout are plentiful in some sections, and surprisingly large in others, though it's rare to find both together.

The Creek

The creek is most notable in my personal history as the place where I finally began to understand nymph fishing. Among the small rocky pools and short gravelly runs, I came to realise that nymphing was actually a good way of catching trout, instead of merely an elaborate test prescribed by the wise old men of fly-fishing.

When I lived in Melbourne, this creek was the one I tended to visit ahead of others. With frequent trips I gained some understanding of its idiosyncrasies. As you begin to understand a water, you naturally want to put that understanding to good use. And so I find myself looking back nearly twenty years on what must be over a hundred trips to this otherwise unremarkable stream.

Ironically, since moving much closer to the creek, I have come to visit it less, and for the last few years, hardly at all. This period coincided with prolonged drought. Many streams in central Victoria suffered terribly during this period, and to be honest, I had left the creek alone for fear of what I might – or might not – find. Then conditions improved in the district. The autumn break came early, and when the rain was followed by a week of soft, blue April weather, I decided it was time to revisit my old friend.

The creek was low and clear at the first bridge, but clumps of drying frogs blanket tangled in the bankside grass showed that there had indeed been a recent fresh. I stepped from the car for a closer assessment, and where slashes of light cut across the water from a hazy sun, I saw three small trout dart from my shadow. Encouraging. At the next lane downstream, I turned in and parked the car on a small clearing of newly shot grass.

This particular section of the creek was something of a gamble, falling into the 'fewer trout, but bigger' category. If the stream were still in recovery, this part of it might be yet to recruit a viable population of fish. A short walk brought me to the edge of a deeper pool. At once, two frightened ducks cut a foaming gash up the middle. Yet under the yellowing willow right at the head, I saw an unconcerned rise. Sensing an early opportunity, I strode up the bank, but in a few steps I scared another fish, which bow-waved straight for the willow at the top. A minor commotion in the shadows suggested that both fish were now spooked. However, any sense of disappointment was masked by delight at finding two good fish in the first few metres.

I fished poorly for the next couple of hours. A summer on the big mountain rivers had dulled my finesse. I continually forgot to check my back cast, which resulted in frequent hook-ups on willows and furze-covered banks. On small streams, the first cast is often the only one that counts. By the time I had put down the rod and walked back to retrieve my fly from the undergrowth, any chance at the trout in question was usually gone. Either it saw me as I stumbled around, or else it had moved by the time I was in position again. Once lost sight of, these fish are rarely caught.

It wasn't just a lack of practice, though, that tarnished

The Creek

my skills. I found myself being swept up by sheer boyish delight at being back on the creek. On a stream where patience and calm bring success, exuberance costs fish. And of course with every trout I saw, the bounce in my step increased. Despite the passage of years since I had last fished this stretch, I started recognising things long forgotten. Little things mostly, of no great consequence, and yet there was a remarkable comfort in seeing them unchanged by time. That old blackwood with the snapped-off top continued to signal a small but surprisingly deep rock hole beneath it, as it had always done. And a wretched blackberry patch still blocked access along the left bank to the top of what I called the 'tunnel pool'. So just as I had been forced to for nearly twenty years, I had to back-track 50 metres, cross over, and fight my way up through the furze on the right bank. All this for a single cast to the head of the pool . . . but three times over the years that cast had produced a 2-pounder.

It is difficult to explain the sense of wellbeing at finding so little changed – even the annoying bits! With every feature recognised, I was eager to see the next one again. It was a bit like watching a much-enjoyed, but half-forgotten movie. And in my eagerness, I think I fished too fast and too carelessly.

Eventually I came to the Poplar Pool. The grand old guardians of this stretch were just starting to turn towards the singed orange of the season, and the prettiness of the view was enhanced by a solid rise at the base of the closest tree. I moved up towards it, passing the broad, shallow and featureless tail as I did so. Right at the very edge of memory

Call of the River

I sensed the vaguest disquiet . . . and responded too late. From behind the only feature in the tail – a single large rock – a fat trout shot up towards its companion beneath the poplar.

Enough! I'd made one mistake too many. The best water on this stretch ended only 500 metres ahead, so it was time to settle down and fish properly before the chances ran out.

I approached the tail of yet another fine pool, determined to make amends. Well back from the lip, I was already crouched over and using the shadows. This pool had also changed very little. If past experience was any guide, there were sure to be a couple of nice fish finning quietly. They'd be working the snail beds just above the point where the pool spilled into the little rock hole below. The rock hole! Hidden in the shade of a huge willow, and no bigger than a pair of dining tables, I had forgotten it. And now, almost alongside, I recalled that it often held a large fish. But was I too close already? Would my carelessness cost yet another chance? Scarcely daring to breathe, I dropped down onto my elbows and inched backward.

Well back from the hole, I stripped off line for one shot right into the base of the feeding cascade. I allowed a single false cast, then delivered the nymph. It landed in the sweet spot, disappearing at once into a small patch of foam beneath the waterfall. I immediately gave one gentle draw, then another . . . Yank! The nymph was taken hard, and the rod tip dived. There was a glimpse of pale flank in the mottled water . . . Gone! Limp line, the hook had simply pulled.

The Creek

These things happen in fly-fishing. Sometimes fish just come off. There was nothing I could think of that I should have done differently, and anyway I was too excited to feel much loss. At last I had hooked a trout, and probably a very nice one.

I finally landed a fish in the next pool. There were a couple of swirls near the uncluttered right bank. These were plain to see, and could be covered by a straightforward cast. Within moments of the nymph landing, there was an excited boil beside it, and the leader twitched. This foot-long brownie pulled its hardest, but I soon had it on the bank – chubby and colourful. There was relief in actually separating a trout from the water at last, tempered somewhat by the knowledge that the fish was also the easiest opportunity of the afternoon.

In April, the shadows grow long early, and by the time I finished the remainder of the pool, sunlight had left the creek completely, lost behind the dry gums on the hillside. I turned to walk back, hoping for perhaps a second chance at a fish here and there before I reached the car.

I was particularly keen to redeem myself at the Poplar Pool, and this time I stalked the tail as a hunter might sneak up on a grizzly bear. But alas, my patient and delicate casts neither attracted nor frightened anything. The tail was still deserted – no doubt a legacy of my earlier blunders. In fact, most of the stream seemed lifeless, as if the warning sirens of 'fisherman around' still echoed from pool to pool.

Eventually I drew near the car, just out of sight around

the next bend. The easiest path to it lay straight around the hillside through the short, faded grass. Following the creek meant shuffling down through yet another wilderness of furze and blackberry, and two slippery crossings. It hardly seemed worth it. And yet as I took a few steps along the easy route, I hesitated. Sunlight had now left the valley completely, lighting only the tops of the highest hills. There wouldn't be time to fish another destination this evening. If I wanted a final cast, it had to be now. Without any great conviction, I made my way to the creek.

Evening had arrived already in the shadow of blackwoods and willows. It was quiet and dim along the stream, so that a single glance was no longer enough to scan the water. A large pool lay immediately downstream of the point where I reached the creek, and it was necessary to stand and peer carefully at the mirrored surface to be sure of seeing any rises and swirls. And there was a rise. At first as ambiguous as a reflected cloud, but then repeated in more distinct confirmation. A fish was sipping with barely audible clipping sounds at the far extremity of the pool, perhaps 20 metres away. Two more rises moved towards me, and I prepared to cast. But then the trout lazily porpoised away again, back to the tail. In the next few minutes the fish twice appeared to be heading up the pool, yet each time it turned back to busily work the small area furthest from me.

My problem was distance. I had virtually no back-cast room. I couldn't wade towards the trout without sending bow waves everywhere, and the banks on either side were

The Creek

impenetrable. At the far end where the fish spent most of its time, the pool disappeared into a thicket of flood-fallen willows.

With no alternative, I began casting down the pool. The best throw I could manage was about 10 metres – a good two rod-lengths short of the trout's closest position. With each presentation, I vaguely hoped that an unseen trout might take the nymph. But the only fish that showed was my adversary, continuing to circle at a safe distance.

I was contemplating the futility of my efforts, and the fading light, when the rises moved my way once again. I resigned myself to the inevitable turn well beyond casting range, but this time there was a further rise about 2 metres closer. I had just made the best cast I could, and I barely twitched the nymph, hoping the trout would break with tradition and come yet closer. Alas, there were no rises nearer or further. Indeed, for some seconds it seemed that all activity had ceased. Then came the pull on my line hand, totally unexpected, and for once I didn't slip. Instantly the still twilight was shattered as a large brown leapt three times in as many seconds. It would be nice if I could now tell you of my prowess in fighting an unexpectedly large trout in a confined, snaggy pool. But it was only blind luck that saved me during those first moments. The fish moved so fast and erratically that I had no real control. In fact, it wasn't until a few minutes had passed that I began to feel as if I were actually having some positive influence on what was happening.

At last the trout was circling close by, and on one pass I

waded in to get a hand under it. Big mistake. With another burst of energy, it shot straight through my legs and in underneath the blackberry bush behind me. Several hundred dollars worth of fly rod bent at a sickening angle before I had the sense to let the line go slack. With great humility, I put the rod down on a clear bit of bank, and took the line in my hand. Would the prize still be there? It was. Finally tired out, it protested only mildly as I untangled leader and fish from the catacombs beneath the bank.

What a marvellous trout! At least 3 pounds, its condition belied what must have been a tough summer. The trout was a female, and even in the soft half-light, her flanks were yellow–green, and her back generously spotted. The nymph popped out of the top lip with unnerving ease, and she was gone without the need for a steadying hand.

I found a break in the furze bush, and stumbled up the nearest sheep track towards the car, feeling a little giddy and grateful. After all these years, the creek had been kind to me once more. I won't stay away so long next time.

Sixteen

Europe

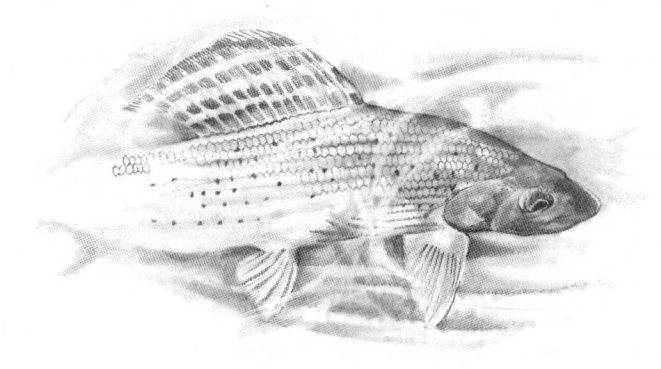

WHEN JANE AND I headed for Europe in July 2001, pursuits other than fly-fishing dominated the itinerary. A couple of weeks were allocated to life in a Tuscan farmhouse, from where we planned to explore quaint hilltop towns, ancient churches and world-famous art. Tentative plans then included a train journey over the Alps to visit Jane's brother in Austria. The final week would be spent touring Denmark with friends.

While no part of our journey was planned with fly-fishing in mind, it will come as no surprise that a four-piece rod, together with a few essentials, were carefully packed in my suitcase. Every country we intended to visit held trout water, and I was quietly confident of at least some opportunities for a cast.

Italy looked as if it might present some of the best chances. While not renowned for its fly-fishing, the mountainous areas of the country still hold trout, including (we were reliably informed) some Tuscan streams. Shortly before our departure from Australia, a friend active in the international fly-fishing scene contacted a prominent Italian fly-fisher on my behalf. All sorts of generous offers of assistance were made. But when I tried the suggested phone numbers on arrival in Tuscany, either no one answered, or I met with the telephone equivalent of a bored shrug.

Further enquiries also went nowhere. Perhaps I was unlucky in my choice of contacts. It seemed that recreational fishing, let alone fly-fishing, was only the vaguest of concepts among the local population. Despite the bilingual powers of our kind hosts, Pat and Geoff, bemused looks or half-forgotten childhood anecdotes were all I could glean from Italian friends and acquaintances. As for questions about trout, I came to the disheartening conclusion that no-one really knew what they were, never mind where they could be found.

In the end, I was left to my own devices to try to hunt down the mythical Italian trout. A few streams glimpsed near our farmhouse base seemed to have potential, but closer inspection found them too warm for trout (the

Tuscan summer is consistently hot) and dominated by small, carp-like fish.

Then one morning, Pat and Geoff announced a visit to the adjacent province of Umbria to explore the famous caves of Grotte di Frassi. I silently noted that this trip would also offer the opportunity to reconnoitre some very trouty-looking country.

However, it was hard to ignore the promise of the caves themselves. The guidebook explained that they were discovered only recently by some young hikers, out exploring the jagged limestone mountains around the Sentino River. During a break, one of these hikers noticed a cool breeze emanating from a small hole in the ground. Suspecting a hidden cave, they dropped a stone into it to test the depth. About ten seconds passed before it clanged to the bottom. They had discovered one of the largest underground caverns in Europe – big enough to contain the Milan Cathedral.

We arrived at the caves around midday after a leisurely two-hour drive. All thoughts of trout and fishing were temporarily banished as we explored this limestone wonderland. A marvellous job has been done of constructing a safe, footsure pathway through the underground maze of secret passages, transparent lakes and gaping caverns. In contrast to some caves, the Caves of Frasassi are lit using simple white light: the natural colours and formations are left to display their own subtle beauty, instead of being bathed in garish reds and blues.

In the quiet damp of a constant 13 degrees, our English-speaking guide pointed out the various features in a musical accent that seemed perfectly matched to our surroundings. She explained the painstaking growth of the stalactites and stalagmites, and the variations in colour from purest ice-white, to rusty red. The one-hour tour was over too soon. For all the magnificence of the great churches and cathedrals we were to visit during our time in Italy, nothing equalled the Caves of Frasassi.

Emerging into the glaring sunlight and 30-degree heat, the sound of the nearby Sentino River caught my attention, and the spell of the caves was broken. Glimpses from the road earlier had suggested a possible trout stream, clear and fast flowing in a narrow gorge, and surrounded by 1500-metre mountains. I clambered down a steep slope towards the stream, excited by the sight of large fish gliding through the water. Were they – ? No. When I got close enough, I could see that the troutish profiles belonged to large roach-like fish that chose to graze on the rock algae, while ignoring the insects that drifted by.

On the road home, the Sentino gradually shrunk as we followed it upstream through a narrow, chalk-walled chasm. At the last bridge before the road swept away, the valley briefly broadened and I asked Geoff to halt the car. I crept down through the willows to a riffly stream no more than 3 metres wide. There was a small, flat pool directly beneath the bridge, and as I peered out from the bushes to view it better, a small rainbow darted from a boulder directly beneath me. An Italian trout at last! However, signs containing the words *'pesca'* and *'vietare'* lined parts of the stream, so I dared not unpack the rod without deciphering them. First glance at my Italian/English dictionary gave the words 'peach' and 'forbidden'. Phew! It was only forbidden to pick the peaches! But then a closer inspection revealed a second meaning for the word *'pesca'*: fishing. With a resigned sigh, I walked back to the car, leaving that solitary Sentino trout to feed in peace.

Deciding that Italian trout fishing was about as probable as a cheap restaurant in Florence, I determined to set my sights a little lower. Not far south of our farmhouse lay the vast Lake Trasimeno. This natural, circular lake is the largest body of water in central Italy, measuring tens of kilometres in diameter. Though reputed to be a reasonable fishery, the lake is most famous for another reason: it is the site of one of the worst defeats of the Roman Army. In Italy, you are never far away from reminders of a complex and ancient past. It seemed somehow appropriate that I could not even go fishing without encroaching on a significant historical site.

In the year 217 BC, Lake Trasimeno was even larger than it is today, and it stretched farther back towards the oak-covered hills. Around this time, the exiled Carthagian prince Hannibal had spent several years roaming through what is now Spain and France, gathering an army for a revenge attack against mighty Rome. For their part, the Romans had intelligence of Hannibal's successful crossing of the Alps, and his march south towards the Empire's heart.

A massive Roman garrison numbering in excess of 20,000 men, under the command of the invincible Consul Caius Flavius, marched north to deal with this elephant-riding upstart from Africa. However, when Flavius made camp on the north shore of Trasimeno several days later, he had gravely misjudged the speed of Hannibal's progress. Expecting the enemy to still be hundreds of kilometres north, Flavius hadn't bothered to send scouts ahead. The Carthagian made no such mistake, and his spies soon located the massive Roman camp, set with virtually no guards on a smallish flat between the lake and the hills. Under cover of dawn mists, Hannibal's army swept down upon the sleeping Romans. In the ensuing battle, 16,000 centurions perished, many driven into the lake half-dressed in armour, where they drowned. Hannibal lost a mere 2000 men. After the fight was won, Hannibal rounded up the few thousand surviving Romans and enlisted them to bury his dead troops.

And here's the part I find most incredible. Hannibal, whose home country had been brutally invaded by the very Romans he had just defeated, and who lived in an age not known for its mercy on any side, simply let the captives go. No ransoms, no killing, no slaves.

I found myself not far from the battleground 2218 years later, but with far less dramatic intentions: catching a fish in Italy on the fly. While Trasimeno's summer water temperatures and lack of depth make it unsuitable for trout, the locals assured me that it teemed with other fine species. Some of these basked in such glorious titles as Queenfish and Regentfish, which sounded promising until I was proudly shown one of these 'Queenfish'. A gift to our hosts, it was actually a European carp. Unfortunately, this same fish was earmarked for the farmhouse dinner table. I did my best to hide dismay at this prospect, quietly hoping that some unknown genetic feature of Italian carp, or some ingredient in Pat's recipe, would render the carp edible. Sadly not: unlike most Tuscan produce, the carp taste just as revolting as their cousins on the other side of the world.

With my expectations for fishing excitement suitably lowered, I nevertheless wandered down to the lake, picked a bead-head Tom Jones from the fly box and started casting. As one of my favourite prospecting wets, the bead-head Tom Jones is also my 'Don't know where else to start' fly on unfamiliar water. It is surprising how often it works. After about half an hour wading the lukewarm, weedy shallows of Trasimeno, I spotted some swirls, then some silver flashes beneath the greyishly clear water.

I stripped the Tom Jones through the area and was rewarded at once with a solid pull, and the sight of a silvery shape fighting against the line. The 8-inch fish was soon brought to shore, where it revealed itself as a sort of cross between a mullet and a baby tarpon.

For the next twenty minutes or so, every cast brought a slashing response from one of these fish, though mostly they failed to hook up. I ended up landing five up to a foot long before the activity moved further out into the lake and beyond casting range. There was a mild satisfaction in finally catching some fish on the fly in Italy. Yet the modest, large-scaled fish did not inspire an eager search for more. I folded up the rod and headed back for a cappuccino at the nearest lakeside cafe.

Our trip to Austria was the most haphazardly planned part of the European tour; final arrangements were not put in place until a few days before our departure. This last-minute planning also appeared to scuttle any opportunities for fly-fishing. Our Austrian destination was the little town of Gruenau, where Jane's brother Angus was helping to run a hostel. Upon learning of our intentions to visit, Angus had kindly done some research on my behalf, only to discover most fishing permits for the district had already been booked soon after the season opened. It turned out we should have tried to obtain a permit weeks earlier, but at that stage our plans for Austria were unknown anyway.

Resigned to admiring any Austrian trout from afar, I departed Florence station for the ten-hour train ride north minus my fly rod. I was disappointed, but the sting was mitigated by thoughts of indulging another love: exploring mountains. Jane's descriptions from a previous visit promised great things.

The night train from Florence crossed the Brenner Pass just as the first faint glow of daybreak silhouetted the surrounding mountains – or at least that's what I discovered when I pushed my face against the window and looked straight up. As the light increased, so did the detail of the landscape. Overnight rain had apparently cleared not long before, leaving behind wet roofs and lanes on the tiny valley farms, and scarves of mist clinging stubbornly to the steep, fir-covered slopes above. Higher still, bare rock and hardy pasture fought with each other for space. And then in the very sky overhead, more than 3000 metres above sea level, midsummer snow filled the ravines and avalanche chutes that scaffolded bush-saw peaks.

At Kufstein, we changed trains and had an hour to kill. If you ever have to wait for a train, Kufstein is the place to do it. Not a hundred metres from the station, the mighty Inn River rumbles through the town centre. The bridge over the river provides a wonderful viewing platform from which to observe this picture-book town, and the massive mountains that crowd against it. However, the Inn itself is what transfixed me – and for once, not because of fishing potential. The sheer volume of the glacier-milk current, visibly sloping downhill to the west, looked as if it had broken free of a shattered upstream dam. In fact, the locals told me that this was low summer level. 'You should see it during the spring thaw,' they said, pointing to the concrete barrier walls rising 8 metres above the water on both banks.

It seemed we barely had time to glimpse Kufstein before the train to our next stop, Wels, arrived. The railway line continued to follow the Inn valley, which gradually widened until the mountains no longer loomed above us. Instead they formed a scenic backdrop to a mixture of dark forest and emerald farmland. The countryside became tamer the further east we went, until the train was speeding through a tidy lushness of small farms, woodland patches and neat villages.

At Wels, we changed for the final time, boarding a quaint single-carriage diesel that looked like a toy after the slick inter-continental electric which had carried us this far. Right on the promised dot of 11.03 am, the little locomotive gave a toot, departed with Austrian punctuality, and headed south at modest speed towards our ultimate destination of Gruenau. The single set of tracks and gentle pace lent a rural intimacy to the journey. Despite the frequent farmhouses and tiny towns, scattered woods evidently provided shelter to abundant wildlife. Pheasants flew clumsily from beside the tracks, while hares played careless games in fields of stubble. Even an occasional wild deer could be seen, bobbing away from the train in the midst of thick, unharvested crops.

The distant jaggedness of the mountains grew closer with every kilometre, and eventually we left the rolling hills altogether and entered the Alm River valley. Farmland still prospered on the valley floor, but the slopes were suddenly too steep for agriculture, returning to the alpine mix of rock cliffs and fir forest we had last seen back toward Kufstein. Then the Alm River itself came into view.

I've seen plenty of rivers in my life, yet I can't think of any that look more idyllic than the Alm. About 20 or 30 metres wide, the river flows determinedly (but not chaotically) over a bed of pale gravel. This substrate momentarily makes the stream appear as a cloudy glacial river. Then you realise the water is actually so pure, the stream *bed* appears as the colour of the water itself.

As if to tantalise, the rail line closely followed the west bank of the Alm. So near was the river, so clear was the water and so leisurely the train's pace, that I began to see trout. Not just rises and swirls – actual trout, finning quietly in the sun-lit current. In every likely place there were five or six. They were nice stream fish, maybe a pound or more. Yet these were effectively forbidden trout. I was like a beggar at a bakery window.

Angus met us at Gruenau station, and we drove the final minutes to the hostel. Located among a tall forest of birch and spruce, and surrounded by near-vertical peaks, Angus's home was the very definition of an Austrian lodge. A tributary of the Alm chattered past a few a metres away. I strolled down to admire it, spotting three small rainbows instantly.

Angus wandered down to offer a beer. 'Well, I've got some news,' he announced. 'I didn't think it would be possible, but I've been able to get you a permit to fish the Alm. Jorg from the hotel in town has offered one of his.' Angus went on to explain the details, while I stood there mouth agape. The large hotels buy up most of the best permits at the beginning of each season for their guests. Apparently the owner of the main hotel in Gruenau had heard of my plight, and offered me a permit from his own stock, even though I was not a guest and we had never met! It was an example of the extraordinary generosity and hospitality of the Austrians, a trait I was already recognising after less than twenty-four hours in their country.

Yet this unexpected news left me torn between elation and disappointment, for while I now had the coveted permit, all my fishing equipment was back in Italy. No problem! Gerhart, the owner of the hostel, was soon on the phone to various contacts. After three calls, he triumphantly announced that he had located a fly-fisher in town who was only too happy to lend his best equipment to a total stranger from Australia.

The following morning, Gerhart drove me to meet my benefactor. Johann (call me John) met us in front of his fishing-gear-filled garage, along with his fly-fishing daughter Johanna. John was a member of the local fly club, and effectively the caretaker of the several kilometres of the Alm I was entitled to fish (and yes, it was the same stretch I viewed from the train). Well, the international code of fly-fishers kicked in at once, and we were soon babbling away like old mates. Fortunately, John's excellent grasp of English was many times better than my pitiful knowledge of Austrian. Occasionally though, we would stumble on an unfamiliar word. Never mind! A burst of mime, often involving a casting motion followed by vigorous pointing at various bits of equipment, soon resolved all communication problems.

I signed my permit, solemnly read the regulations John had provided in English, and then received a rod and reel very similar to my own outfit. I bade John a heartfelt farewell; however, to my delight he asked if it would be all right if he joined me a little later.

That first hour on the river was magical. I began by following a neat path that traced the stream from just behind a screen of beech and willow. John had described a certain bend that I should head to, but after three or four delectable pools I could stand the strain no longer, and cut through to the water. I could hardly believe my good fortune. Less than a day after helplessly viewing all those fish from a train window, I was now right among them, heavily armed with rod and flies.

Every few hundred metres the flow of the Alm is interrupted by a small weir. Mostly, these divert some of the current down a bankside aqueduct, which then returns to the river via a steep drop and a hydro-electric turbine. It's all unobtrusive, clean, and a great way to generate power with a minimum of environmental impact.

I had reached the river not far below one such weir, and as I made my way upstream, the flow on the right bank slowly narrowed into an inverted V-shape, bounded on one side by the angular, cascading weir, and on the other by the natural bank. I scared several fish from the smooth water downstream with alarming ease. One of John's main points was emphasised – these were obviously wild fish, not stupid stockies. However as I neared the top of the inverted V, the surface became more agitated. Perhaps any fish present would be less easily frightened. From the cover of a toppled beech branch I stared into the flickering current windows, trying to muster my New Zealand trout polaroiding skills, for the conditions were almost identical.

As my eyes adapted to the features of the little piece of water, I discovered two 'rocks' which appeared to move around more than could be explained by current cycles alone. One was smallish, but the other looked to be a good size. I presented a bead-head nymph several times, but neither shape responded. Though it was still early, and the conditions cool and overcast, I changed the nymph for a white-winged CDC dry (size 16) which John had recommended. The first cast was wide, but the second drifted right over the quivering shapes, and the larger of the two hovered backward beneath the fly. In the illusively clear water, the fish did not appear to come high enough to take my offering, but suddenly there was a rise anyway, and I struck wildly.

The rod bent, there was a clear view of an extraordinary blue and cream marbled flank . . . and then nothing. My first Alm fish, probably an Arctic char, was gone. I was aware the river offered the chance of at least five species of sportfish: brook trout, Arctic char, rainbow trout, brown trout and grayling. Still, until that flash of blue and cream, I had subconsciously expected the usual brown and rainbow mix of home.

Encouraged by the response to the dry, I persisted with it. Just above the weir, several fish rose periodically to something invisible. They all looked like small ones, except for a couple that fed beneath the trees on the far bank. I waded about a third of the way across the river, teeth gritted against the 12-degree water, and cast just upstream of the trees. The first cast was too far up and the line bowed, dragging the fly before it drifted over the hot spot. The next was better, and just before the fly began to skate, a fawn shape materialised beneath it. Snip! The CDC was gone. This time the strike was better timed, and a fat, pan-sized rainbow stayed attached. It pulled with the vigour cold water seems to encourage in trout, and I was careful, given the unknown breaking strain of the fine tippet John had supplied. However everything held together, and shortly I had my first Austrian trout on the bank.

John and his daughter joined me soon after. While Johanna fished down and across below us, we persisted with dry flies. My companion and his insulating neoprenes took the deep water on the far bank. I gratefully settled for the near side of the run, where my sandalled feet could slowly adjusting to the chilly flow. By now the air itself was almost muggy, and John felt conditions were perfect for action, and perhaps even a genuine hatch.

The seam on my side of the run looked fairly unspectacular, with only half a metre of water over a uniform bed. I could polaroid the fuzzy shapes of several modest targets. Yet as I had found in the quieter water below the weir, each cast – no matter how delicate – sent previously unnoticed fish fleeing, sparking a chain reaction. I was wondering whether it might be better to move straight up to more turbulent water when the fly was suddenly gone in a fast rise.

Europe

Even as I struck, the fish felt different. It swooped down and across the river towards John's position, and he pointed excitedly, mouthing something I couldn't interpret above the noise of the current. After its initial run, the fish was soon lying quietly in the gravelly shallows.

With its out-sized dorsal, and subtly iridescent colours, I recognised my prize only from pictures I had seen in books. 'Congratulations,' beamed John as he splashed forward with outstretched hand. 'A grayling!' My friend had caught just one grayling all season, and he considered these fish a special capture on the Alm. Evidently, I was blessed to catch one within an hour or so of my arrival.

I should point out here that my day on the Alm coincided with John's wedding anniversary, and so our fishing together was interrupted a couple of times while he dashed dutifully home! And as much as I enjoyed having the company of an experienced and enthusiastic host, it was also great to have some time alone on this magnificent stream. In Australia, we think nothing of being by ourselves on the water, where solitude can be bought for the price of a fifteen-minute stroll, or even a trip timed to coincide with a week day. Europe offers space of this kind only rarely.

Yet fishing access to the Alm is limited, and on 'my' stretch this day, I was the only angler. I briefly tasted, in places, the wildness of a Europe mostly lost hundreds of years earlier. With roads and houses screened by trees, and the darkly forested slopes rising endlessly upward all around, it was just me and the hiss and chatter of a perfect river. For a while I could be lulled into fly-fishing's happy trance; dimly aware of the extraordinary surroundings, while completely absorbed with the drift of the fly and the hiding places of fish.

As the day wore on, insect activity multiplied under the increasingly sullen and windless sky. Small drab mayfly bobbed down the riffles, but large olive caddis were more plentiful, and attracted slashing rises from the trout. The grayling were all but invisible on the riverbed, the faintest of silver–grey shimmer. Char and brown trout were darker in colour and relatively speaking, easier to see. But they too hugged the bottom, and were not obvious unless searched for.

Rainbows were the most visibly active species, and at times almost painfully obvious, like birds in a light mist. Yet as with trout the world over, the biggest ones occupied the smartest stations. The hot spot was invariably the 'eye' on the deep side of the river. Often overhung with branches, and inaccessible from the comfortable bank, these places offered the dual obstacles of requiring pinpoint casting, and almost instant drag.

The 16- to 18-inch rainbows that hovered in the eyes *looked* tantalisingly easy. In reality, most coolly faded into the shadows after a couple of unnatural fly drifts, or else utterly ignored subsequent presentations. In one such place, however, I finally managed to tiptoe out on a submerged rock bar to within a short cast of a regular riser. With less conflicting current to contend with, I achieved a metre or so of natural drift, and my target was quick enough to suck down an Elk Hair Caddis before it dragged. In moments, I was trying to teeter back to dry land, while simultaneously managing a well-conditioned trout, hell-bent on making it down to the next weir. What a fighter that rainbow was! At a fat 16 inches, it probably weighed less than 2 pounds, and yet I feared for my newly attached 5-pound tippet right up until I had the fish on the bank.

A short time later I accounted for a couple more rainbows of around a foot, and they proved to be little powerhouses as well. Though some Alm rainbows were inexplicably slabby, the stockier versions were as strong, pound for pound, as any trout I've had on my line.

John joined me again midafternoon, and took great pleasure in driving me to some of his favourite beats. He had marked me as a 'grayling man' and showed me the spots – usually turbulent and deep – where he guessed the best ones to be. Some of these were right in the middle of small towns. How strange to be surrounded by pedestrians, cars and the general activity of village life, and yet to have the river to ourselves.

My companion's faith was more than rewarded as I went on to land a further seven grayling, some around 16 inches. John doubled his season tally by landing one! This was success to the point of embarrassment for me, but I couldn't figure out what was causing it. John was doing the hospitable thing and placing me on the finest spots, yet he was a skilful angler as well. Had I chanced upon a red-letter grayling day, and then got to fish the very best places? Maybe, yet that hardly explains how I, a total grayling novice, managed to land more than a season's worth of these fish in a single day. In hindsight, I wonder if my fast strike (usually a liability) had helped me to combat the super-quick takes of the grayling. Even so, I'm still puzzled at the extent of my luck, though I was very happy to accept it.

Again, the interests of marital harmony called John away from the river. Content with my results, and keen for a short break, I followed. I was treated to a rushed tour of John's private trout farm, set on an icy spring creek and entirely natural save for screens and a couple of side bays for fry rearing. Here was surely the 'hackle on the fly' for a man who lived within walking distance of one of the finest trout streams imaginable. I was instructed to dangle a piece of fish gut from my fingers over a shadowy pool, whereupon 20 inches of Arctic char shot out from under the jetty and snatched it, just missing my fingertips. My startled recoil brought a delighted chuckle from John – evidently I wasn't the first fisher to meet one of his pets!

Finally, we wandered back to the house and it was time to say goodbye, but not before John ceremoniously produced a beautiful little pewter badge featuring a leaping grayling. 'You are the grayling man now,' he announced with a grin. 'With this you can always remember the Alm and her graylings.' The badge has adorned my fishing hat ever since.

I walked alone down the path from John's house to the stream through a canopy of beech and alder. The long-threatened rain was falling at last, just enough to drip occasionally from the sheltering trees. Jane and Angus were due to collect me at dusk, but I had two more hours yet on the precious Alm. I persisted with the dry at first, catching a couple of small rainbows. As the rain became more constant, though, I changed to a nymph for the first time since the start of the day.

At the tumbling head of the pool, I pitched a weighted caddis grub into the seam and it sank quickly. On the third cast, just as I mended, I felt a faint resistance and lifted. A fine brown kicked away in the depths, reluctant to come to the bright surface for some minutes. As with the best rainbows, the fish was not so much long as fat, and as I lifted it for release, I was surprised by the weight. But most striking was the belly colour – truly buttercup yellow. I can't recall a prettier brown trout, and I wished my camera wasn't up under the bridge out of the rain, for I dearly wanted a picture. Two flicks later I caught another brown of the same size, though normal in colour.

By the time I reached the final pool before the meeting place at the road bridge, the rain was coming down hard, and the fish had gone quiet. I worked quickly upriver, keen to reach the shelter of the bridge. Immediately downstream of the pylons, a large tributary entered from the left, tumbling over granite boulders into the main flow. At the junction, a swirling eddy looked like a promising spot for a cast. I flicked the caddis grub into the edge of the eddy and threw an upstream mend immediately to allow the fly to be vacuumed down. I scarcely had time to finish the mend when the leader cut upstream. There was no need to strike – the fish had effectively hooked itself. It was a matter of merely trying to keep a strong adversary from gaining the swift current below the eddy.

I soon recognised the quivering resistance as somewhat different from a trout, and then a glimpse of gold belly and sail fin confirmed I had hooked another grayling – my first on the nymph. This one equalled the best I had caught earlier, and I smiled as I imagined John shaking his head in disbelief as 'Grayling Man' brought his tally to nine for the day.

The grayling hovered by my feet for some moments after release, and then swam steadily back up toward the eddy, where it seemed to blend with the grey–green stones and vanish. I noticed how wet I was from the rain, and the fact that the chill of the river was no longer compensated for by the warmth of my upper body. I walked the remaining metres to the shelter of the bridge, and waited for Jane and Angus.

After Austria, Denmark looked decidedly flat. Even the Danes joke about the terrain, especially their highest peak, Heaven Mountain, which towers a mighty 170 metres above sea level. And yet the Danish countryside has its own soft appeal, with the modest rolling hills sheltering rich farmland and scattered forests. Though it lies as far north as Alaska, Denmark's climate is moderated by warm ocean currents, and it has more in common with the green fields of England than the rest of Scandinavia. Some say that Tolkien's Shire in *The Lord of the Rings* was partly inspired by Denmark.

The biggest surprise to the angler is the amount of water. As well as an abundance of coastal inlets (optimistically called fjords by the Danes), there are numerous freshwater lakes, and many streams. After my gear-less scare in Austria, I was careful to carry my fishing rod everywhere in Denmark.

Most of our time was spent touring the Jutland Peninsula with our resident friends Peter and Anita, and Peter's enthusiastic 8 year old, Tomas. We started at the northern tip of the peninsula, where we followed local custom by wading out and standing with one foot in the North Sea and the other in the Baltic. Tradition dealt with, I went back to the car and assembled the fly rod for some fishing off the beach. Incredibly by Australian standards, sea-trout can be caught off most of the Danish coastline, instead of being confined to estuaries and river mouths. The beaches of northern Jutland were reputed to be especially good.

I felt decidedly strange, standing on a beach not unlike those found along southern Port Phillip, casting a Tom Jones for trout. After about half an hour, the doubts of the unknown began to plague me. Was I fishing in the right place, at the right time? And anyway, were there *really* trout swimming around in the horizon-breaching vastness of the Baltic Sea? Then suddenly, as the fly emerged from behind a seaweed encrusted boulder, a silvery shape shot out and walloped it. A sea-trout! Not a very big one, but as I brought it towards the shore, all my doubts evaporated. So there were trout out there.

On the very next cast, a flounder took the fly. I never thought I'd catch a trout and a flounder on consecutive casts! On my last flick before I hurried back to join the others, a serious bow wave briefly appeared behind the Tom Jones, then faded away. Was it one of the big sea-trout? I couldn't be sure.

The local literature insisted that evening and into the night were the best times for the resident sea-trout, which grew to 15 pounds and more. I was keen to try for one at the 'proper' hour, but in midsummer the Danish evening doesn't begin until after 10 pm. By the time dinner was finished and stories were being traded over a cosy bar, the thought of a night-time wade in the cold Baltic had lost much of its appeal, not to mention being socially questionable. In the end I never did cast a fly under the long Danish twilight. Instead I had to content myself with imagined happenings as I drifted off to sleep . . . lapping wavelets on the darkened beach, a lighthouse flashing upon the distant headland, and of course me locked in mortal combat with a yard-long sea-trout . . .

During the latter part of the week we moved inland from the coast to stay with Anita's parents in the little township of Brande. To my delight, the guidebook flagged the Brande area as very good for fishing. I was soon down at the local tourism office receiving instructions on where to fish. Most streams and lakes in Denmark are privately owned. However, unlike other parts of Europe, much of the fishing access is obtainable without advanced bookings or having to take part in lotteries. It's merely a question of obtaining a general angling licence (available at any post office), approaching the landowner in question, and paying the requested fee, which is often nominal. It is possible that during peak times, popular streams may be hard to get onto. However this wasn't my experience. We were travelling during the Danish holiday season, yet I had no difficulty accessing great fly water simply by turning up and introducing myself to the owner. The most I paid for a day permit was $10, and one fine fellow insisted I fish his excellent stretch of river for nothing.

Though Denmark's streams lack the grandeur of those in Austria, they certainly have their own magic. Those I fished were effectively medium to large spring creeks, laced with watercress, flowing cold and strong, yet with few if any rapids or cascades. Perhaps the most memorable was the little Brande Stream itself, winding through an open flat of waist-high grass and wildflowers, and overhung by the occasional oak. The valley was bounded by lush, rounded hills and I would not have been surprised to see a hobbit or two frolicking on the slopes.

The stream teemed with small brown trout. After a worrying start when even the fingerlings refused my offerings, I changed to an Orange spinner all the way from Millbrook, and caught trout at once. I even caught grayling; much smaller than those from the Alm, but I'm sure John would have been pleased that Grayling Man was living up to his reputation!

Every so often, a respectable brown of a pound or so could be polaroided, and fishing to these specimens was the highlight of the day. Is there anything better than watching a trout, waving gracefully beside the weeds, suddenly glide over to your little dry and sip it down? A mowed path intersected the Brande at various points, and thoughtfully placed wooden benches lined it. As I rested on one of these, retying my tippet in the hazy sunshine, it was easy to imagine I was on a hallowed English chalkstream. The difference was that I had paid six dollars, not six hundred, for the privilege.

The final Danish stream I fished was the fabled Skjern, said by the books to contain not just brown trout and grayling, but sea-trout and Atlantic salmon as well. In appearance, it was simply a much larger version of the Brande. However, the extra depth and flow made it less intimate than the earlier stream: in all that cover and current, you could walk past a 10-pound salmon and never know it.

Despite the Skjern's inviting appearance, I had just one clear chance at a good fish. As high cloud drifted over the sun ahead of an approaching front, a sprinkling of large fawn duns began to emerge. Within minutes, one was taken by a powerful rise close to my bank. Exercising surprising restraint, I removed the spinner I had been prospecting with and changed it for a big Kosciuszko paradun. The artificial drifted about a foot before it was smacked down by a good fish. I thought the take looked confident, and that I struck correctly, yet I barely felt resistance before the fly sailed harmlessly over my shoulder.

After that, I tackled the river again with new determination for about an hour, but to no avail. Whether it was the incoming cold front, a shortage of fish (which I doubt), or simply a lack of local experience, the water seemed lifeless. Eventually time ran out, and I walked back across the fields to where Anita was waiting to drive me back to our lodgings. The threat of rain did not last, and that evening we were able to enjoy an outdoor barbeque with Anita's family. Amidst the good food and twilight laughter, my mind wandered briefly back to the banks of the Skjern. Would those large duns be hatching in earnest now, pursued in the fading light by huge trout that lay hidden by day?

Not long after, our Danish visit came to an end, and with it our time in Europe. Too soon, Jane and I were encased in a 747, high above the desert mountains of Iran and Afghanistan, flying south-east and away from the setting sun. Twenty brain-fuzzing hours later, we walked out into the cold winter evening at Melbourne airport. There, we were met by our friend and neighbour Raymond, who drove us west towards our house in the country. A shivering Jane was consoled by the promise of a fire crackling in the living-room hearth. The talk soon turned to fishing, and despite my foggy head, I was able to give a reasonably coherent summary of our adventures. In return, Ray offered the latest on the local fishing. 'Modewarre's been all right,' he offered. 'There were some nice fish working the inside of the weedbeds last Sunday.' I mentally dragged myself away from the Alm and the Brande to winter on the Victorian lakes. I was home.

Glossary

artificial	Abbreviation of artificial fly.
CDC	Short for Cul de Cunard feathers. The feathers near a duck's preening gland, which are naturally oiled, and thus ideal for tying dry flies.
dun	The drab-coloured form a sub-adult mayfly takes as it emerges from its nymphal skin. Also used to broadly describe some artificial flies.
fresh	A rise in stream level, usually following rain.
hopper	Grasshopper.
naturals	The real insects, crustaceans and so forth as distinct from the artificial fly.
nymph	Broad term used to describe the juvenile phase of many aquatic and other insect species. Also a generic term for a category of artificial fly.
nymphing	(i) Fishing with an artificial nymph. (ii) Trout feeding on nymphs.
paradun	Category of dun imitation tied using a parachute hackle.
polaroiding	Searching for fish with polarising glasses.
riffle	Shallow, broken water flowing swiftly and evenly over gravel.
rise	(i) The act of a trout taking an insect or fly off the water's surface. (ii) The disturbance (usually a spreading ring) left when a trout takes an insect off the water's surface. (iii) A number of trout taking insects from or near the water's surface.
tippet	Final section of the leader to which the fly is tied (the weakest link in the fly line leader chain).

Acknowledgments

MUCH OF THE inspiration for this book comes from time on the water with others. I won't attempt to list all my fishing companions for fear of missing one. Some will have been met on the preceding pages. But there are others, scarcely mentioned or not at all, who have also contributed in their own way. To all, my sincere thanks.

My wonderful partner, Jane Gardner, has the unenviable task of reading most of my manuscripts in their raw state. She manages to gently consign certain bits to the waste paper pile, while also offering ideas and encouragement.

As a non-angler, Bryony Cosgrove quickly acquainted herself with the fly-fisher's world. I could not have hoped for a more eagle-eyed or sympathetic editor.

Rick Keam was – as always – a reliable source of advice, particularly on matters technical. Meanwhile, Patrick Hughes offered invaluable input, both as one well-versed in the literature of fly-fishing, and simply as a lover of the sport.

The combination of gifted artist and gifted fly-fisher is a rare one. I have fished with Trevor Hawkins several times, and if you think he can draw, you should see him fish – especially on a tight stream like the Moonbah. What a delight it has been to watch the drawings for this book unfold, one by one.

Bill Bachman's photography is widely admired by angler and non-angler alike. When I first saw the cover picture, I knew instantly that it captured the river's call.

Cathy Larsen's inspired design work brought all the elements together to create a fine-looking book, a real tribute to the aesthetics of fly-fishing.

Heidi Marfurt masterfully orchestrated the whole production. I'm very grateful for her constant optimism and positive words.

Finally, special thanks to Steve Vizard for a generous and eloquent foreword. This book could have no better beginning.